CHAMPAK

little fingers

Big Brains

Kindergarten plus

Published in Moonstone
by Rupa Publications India Pvt. Ltd 2023
7/16, Ansari Road, Daryaganj
New Delhi 110002

Sales centres:
Bengaluru Chennai
Hyderabad Jaipur Kathmandu
Kolkata Mumbai Prayagraj

P-ISBN: 978-93-5702-295-8
E-ISBN: 978-93-5702-289-7

Second impression 2025

10 9 8 7 6 5 4 3 2

Printed in India

Skills Covered

Numeracy

- Numbers
- Number names
- Ascending Descending
- Greater and lesser than
- Time
- Money
- Addition
- Subtraction
- Counting
- Missing numbers
- Number values
- More and less

- Identify, recognise and count numbers 1-50.
- Assign values to numbers upto 20. Identify and recognise number names.
- Understand the relationship between numbers and quantities.
- Recognising Indian currency.
- Ability to understand time through o'clock.
- Solve basic math problems of addition and subtraction upto number 9.

EVS

- Modes of Transport
- Animals
- Living and non-living things
- Day and night
- Seasons
- Fruits
- Good habits
- Community helpers
- Float and sink
- Healthy and unhealthy

- The worksheets help children differentiate between daily life concepts.
- Recognise and identify pets, farms, aquatics, and wild animals along with their habitat and their young ones.
- Recognise different community helpers and the tools they use.
- Explore more about seasons ,modes of transport, and fruits.
- Identify between living and non-living things, day and night, healthy and unhealthy.
- Develop good manners, self-discipline, and social skills.

Skills Covered

Cognitive Development

- Maze
- Odd one out
- Match the halves
- Do as directed
- Sequence
- Coding

- Cognitive development refers to a child's capacity to engage in reasoning processes such as comprehension, communication, analysis, evaluation, recall, imagination, and foresight.
- It improves problem-solving abilities, critical thinking skills, hand-eye coordination, and spatial awareness.
- Activities such as coding, maze-solving, direction-following , sequence-ordering, and odd-one-out identification can foster children's logical reasoning, decision-making, and task-oriented skills.
- Nurture a child's intellectual development by fostering critical thinking skills.

Literacy

- Upper and Lower- case
- Two and Three Letter words
- Phonics
- Article
- Unscramble

- Utilizing phonetic education to instruct children on vowel sounds and their combination with consonants to establish word families that enhance proper pronunciation, spelling, and letter-sound correlation.
- Proper usage of articles such as 'a', 'an', and 'the' can contribute to the correct formation of sentences.
- The use of reading comprehension sheets helps in developing reading and listening abilities and advancing language proficiency.
- Understanding and recognising the first sounds of words is a crucial factor in a child's language development.

Pre Math

- Up and down
- Tall and short
- Heavy and light
- Clean and dirty
- Full and empty
- Colour
- Shapes

- Pre-math skills are a critical foundation that a child must have before writing.
- All of these skills contribute to the child's capacity to hold and handle a crayon, as well as the child's ability to attempt to draw, trace, copy and colour.

This is me
I am
years old.
I live in
I want to be
when I grow up.
My friends are:
This is my family
My favourite
TV show
Colour
Food
Book

Find the matching lowercase letter for each uppercase letter

B •	• p
T •	• v
S •	• k
Y •	• y
P •	• b
K •	• t
V •	• s

Circle the odd one out in each row

be go so no

if is in to

at an of as

go in no so

my ox on or

me he it we

start | to | me | at | in | go | my | on | is | no | hi | up | as | of | he | so | by | it | oh | be | am | on | if | we | do | an | end

I can read
2
letter words

Literacy

Merge the vowel and consonant to create two-letter words

a

b ab
c
d
f
g
j
k
l
m
n
p
s
t
x

"a" sound words

-at

bat cat sat mat
pat rat hat fat

-an

ban can fan pan
ran tan van man

-ab

cab dab fab
lab nab tab

-ap

cap gap lap map
nap rap sap tap

-ag

bag lag nag sag
tag wag rag

-an

ban can fan man
pan ran tan van

-ad

bad dad fad had
lad sad mad pad

Underline all the "-am" words

 Sam has a  cat. His name is Pam. Pam is a fat  cat.  Sam has  ham and 

jam.  Sam went to see the  dam. On the way he saw a  ram. He got  yam from the  market.

Find the path using the "-ab" words

cab

map

lab

fab

jam

tap

ham

mop

nab

cap

dab

tab

tar

Pair the rhyming words

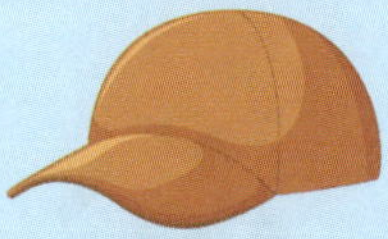

cap

hat

nap

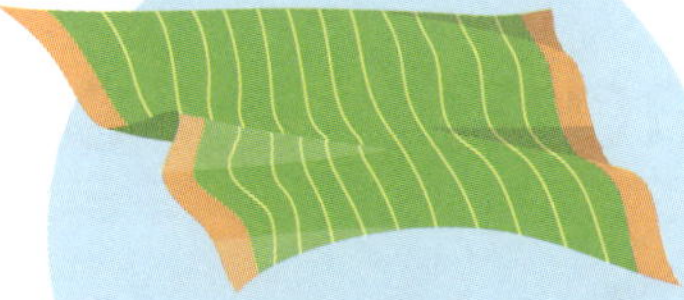

rag

map

tap

gap

mat

lap

bag

Pam kicks only the balls with "-ad" words.
Identify them and circle them.

dad

lad

cab

mad

sad

cap

nap

rap

bad

fad

pan

Literacy

Help the Eskimo reach the igloo using the '-ag' words

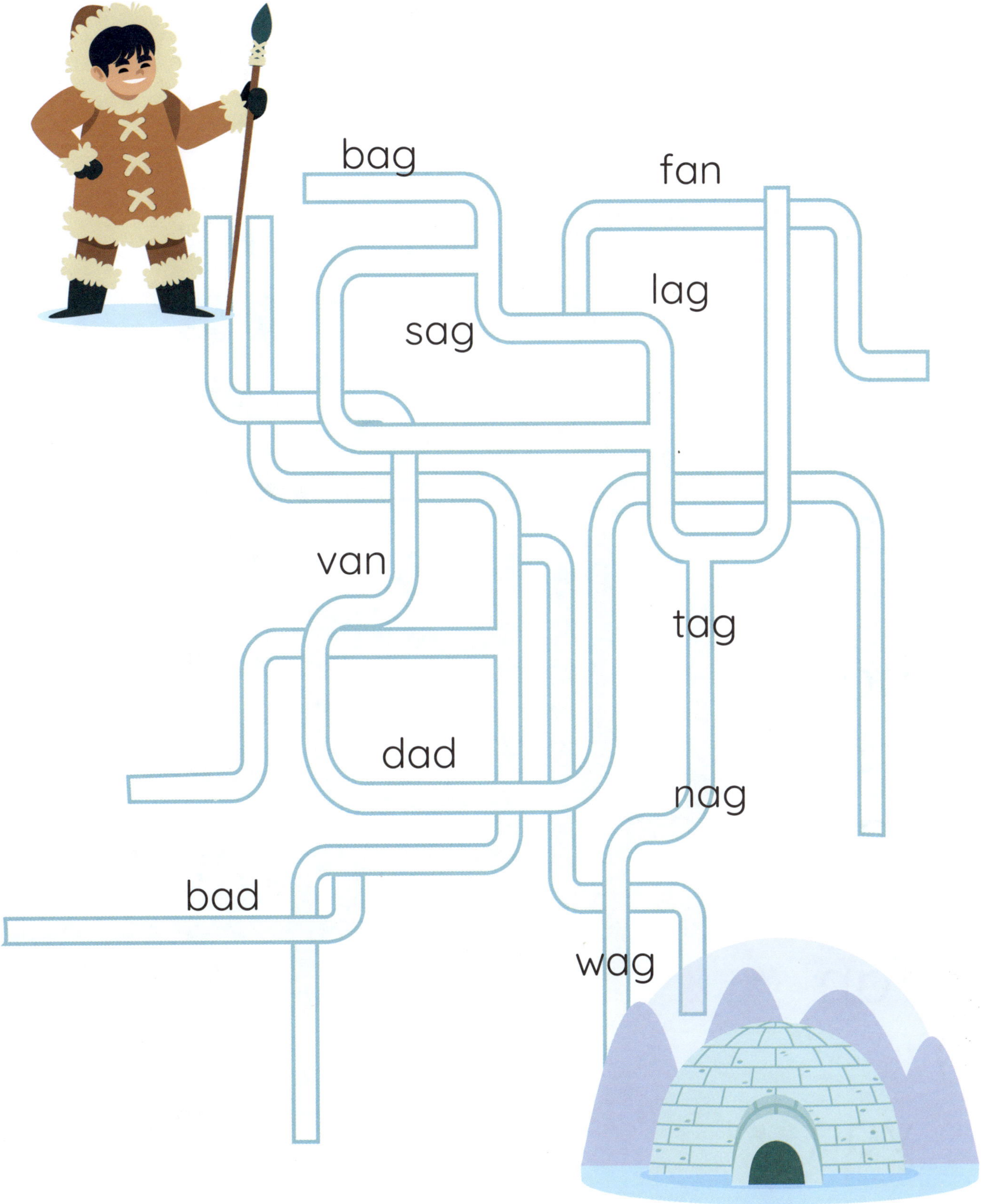
bag
fan
lag
sag
van
tag
dad
nag
bad
wag

Match the words with the pictures

ran •	•
man •	•
pan •	• 
can •	• 
ban •	• 
tan •	• 
fan •	• 
van •	• 

Literacy

Match the words to their objects

bat   mat   cat   rat   hat

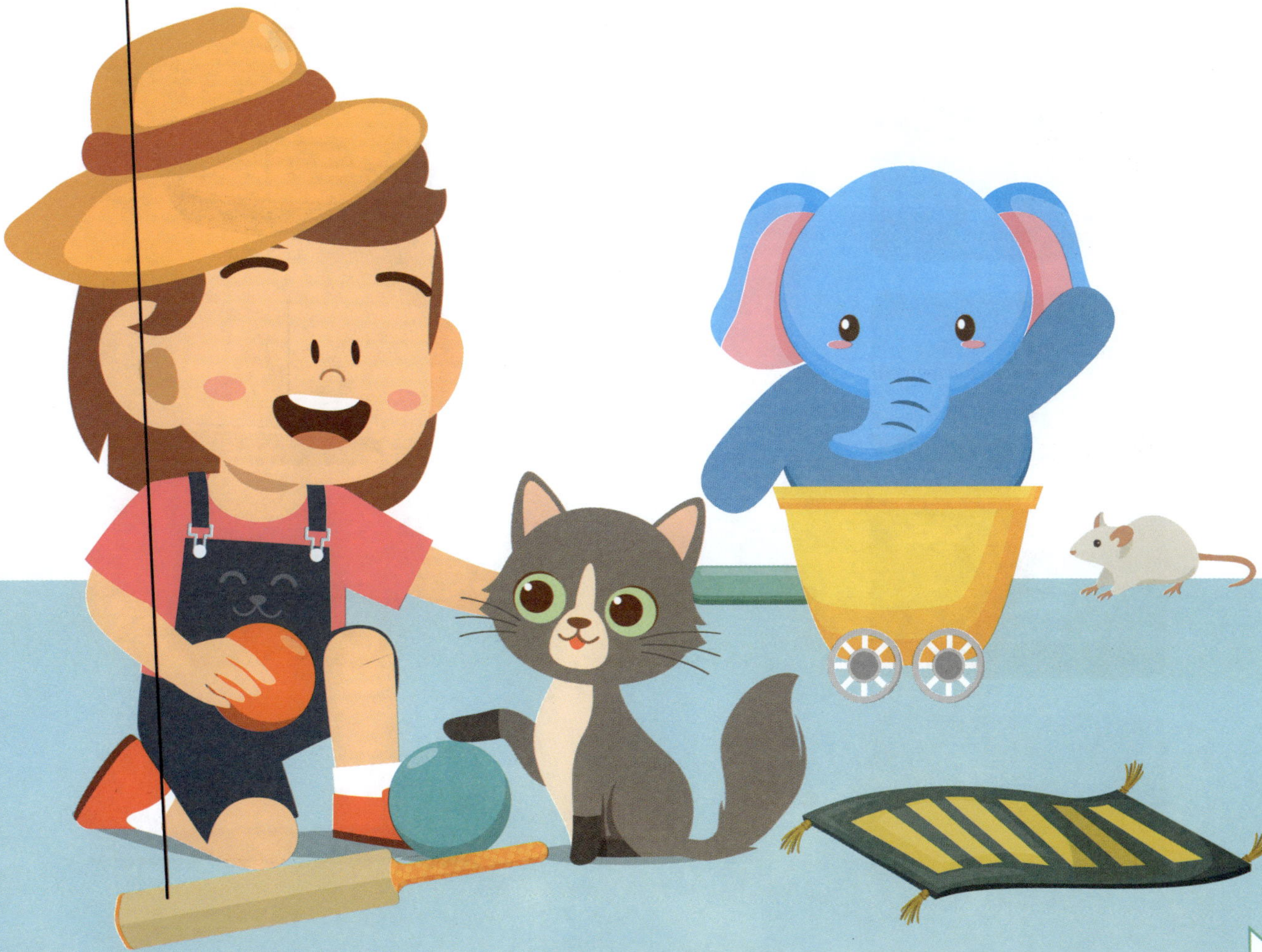

Match the modes of transport to their vehicles

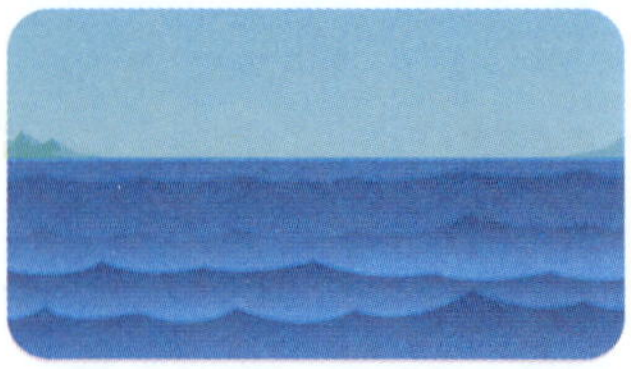

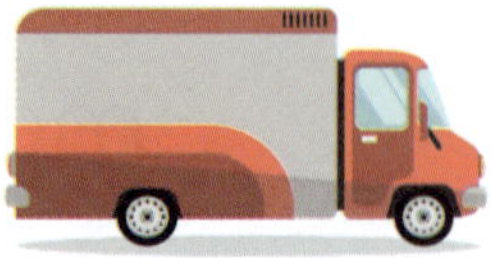

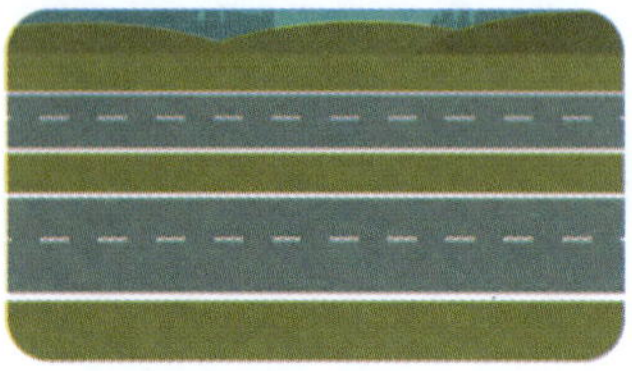

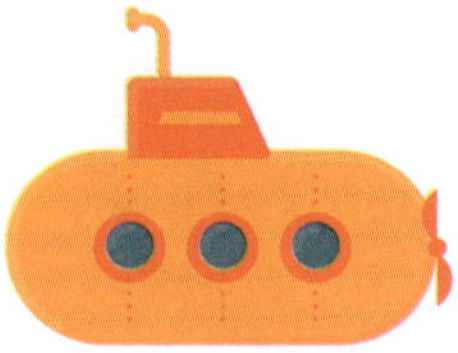

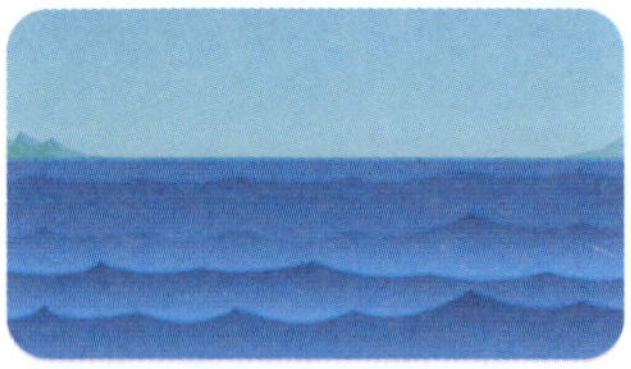

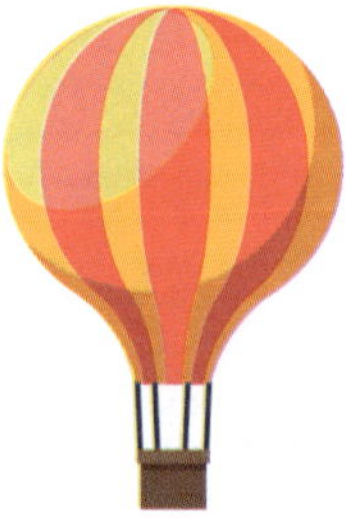

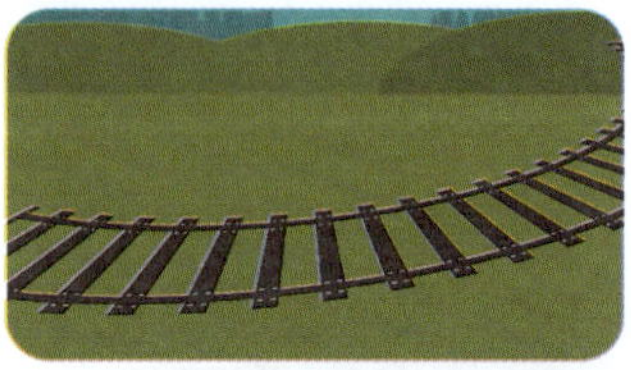

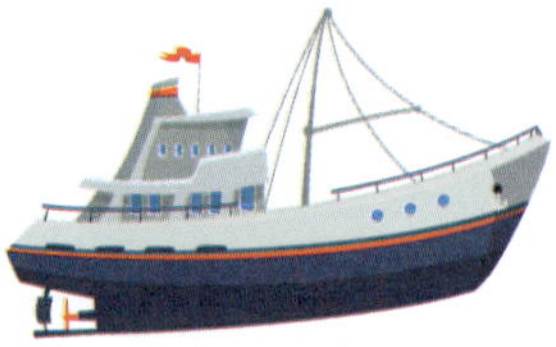

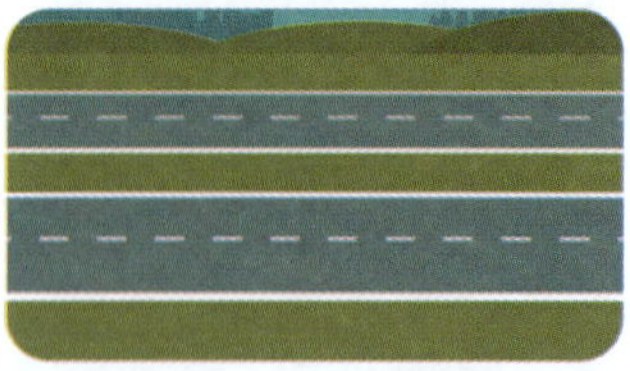

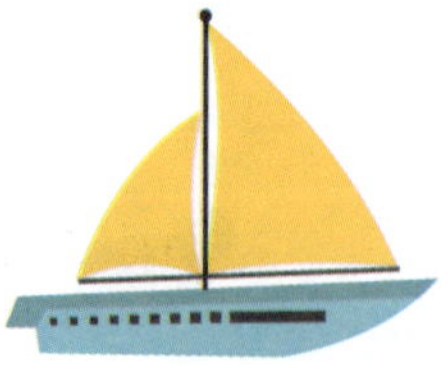

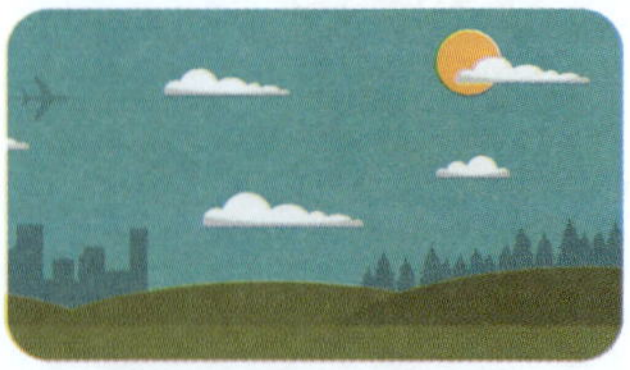

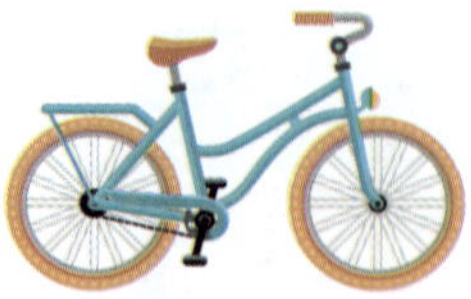

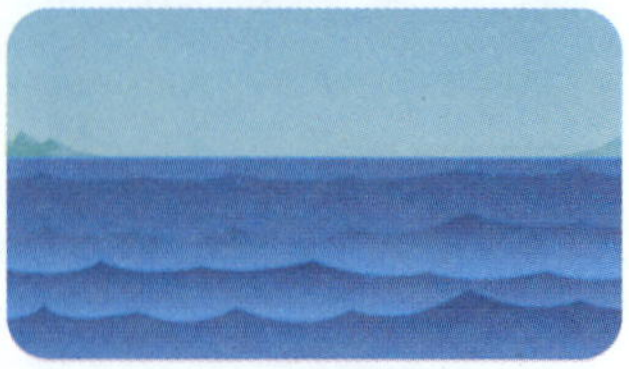

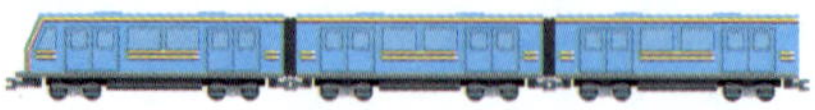

Tick the homes of each animal

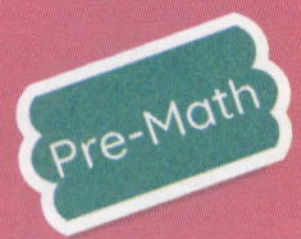

Circle the right direction of the air transport

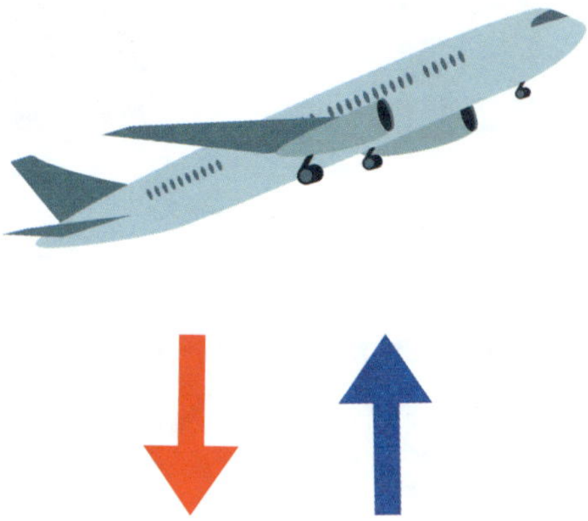

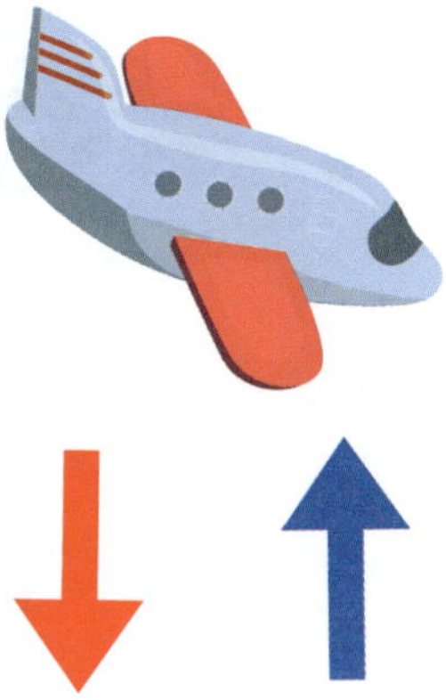

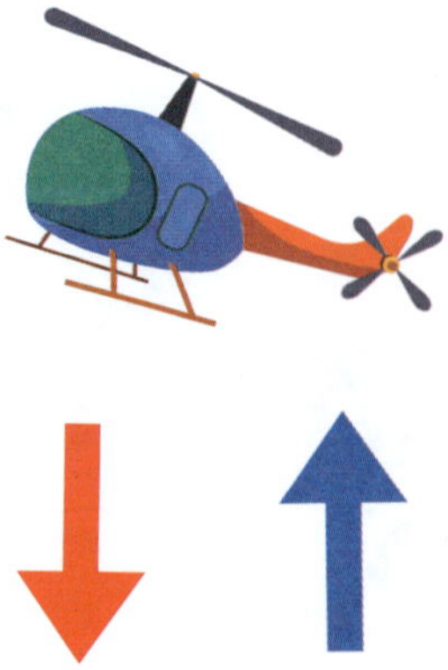

EVS

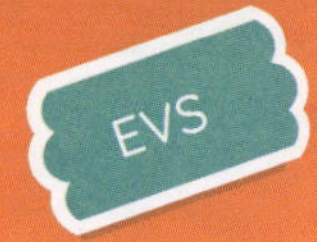

Circle four things that help a plant to grow

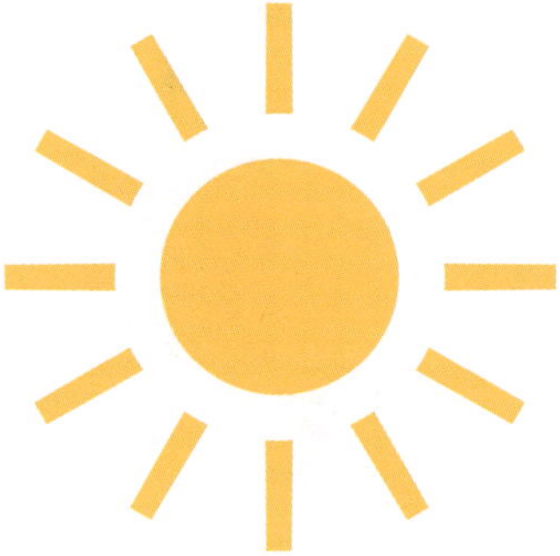

sun

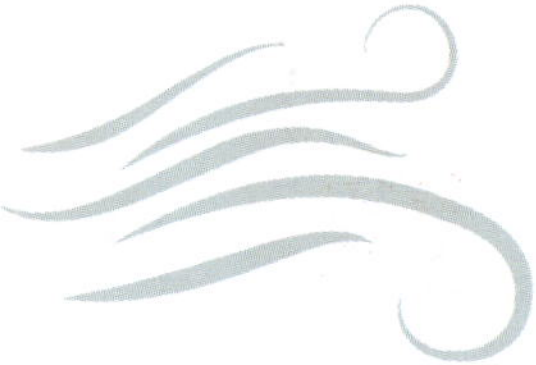

air

cheese

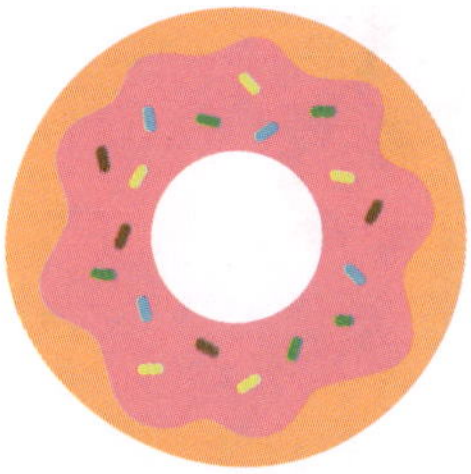

donut

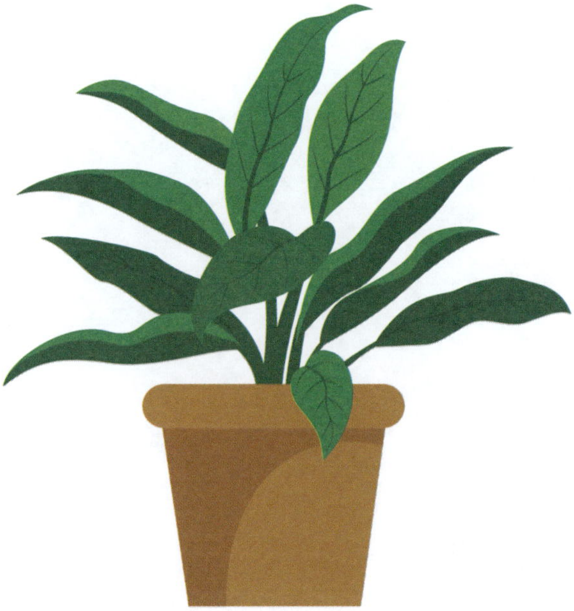

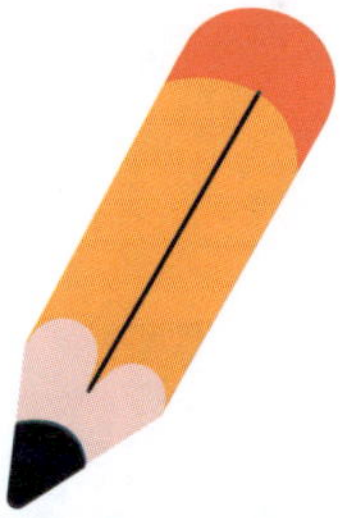

pencil

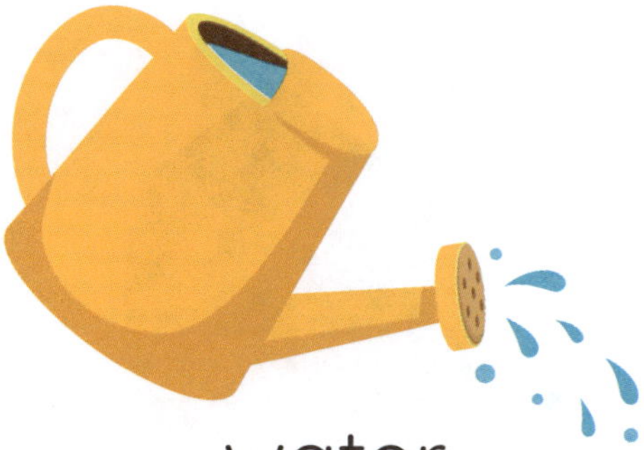

water

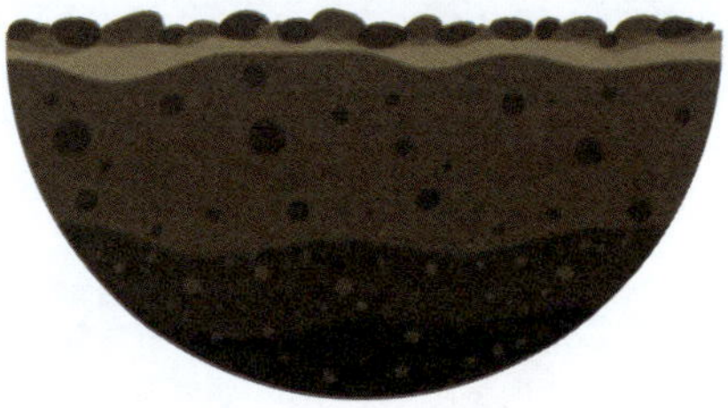

soil with nutrients

Cognitive Development

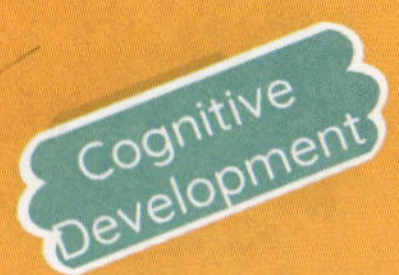

Connect the shapes to their respective towers

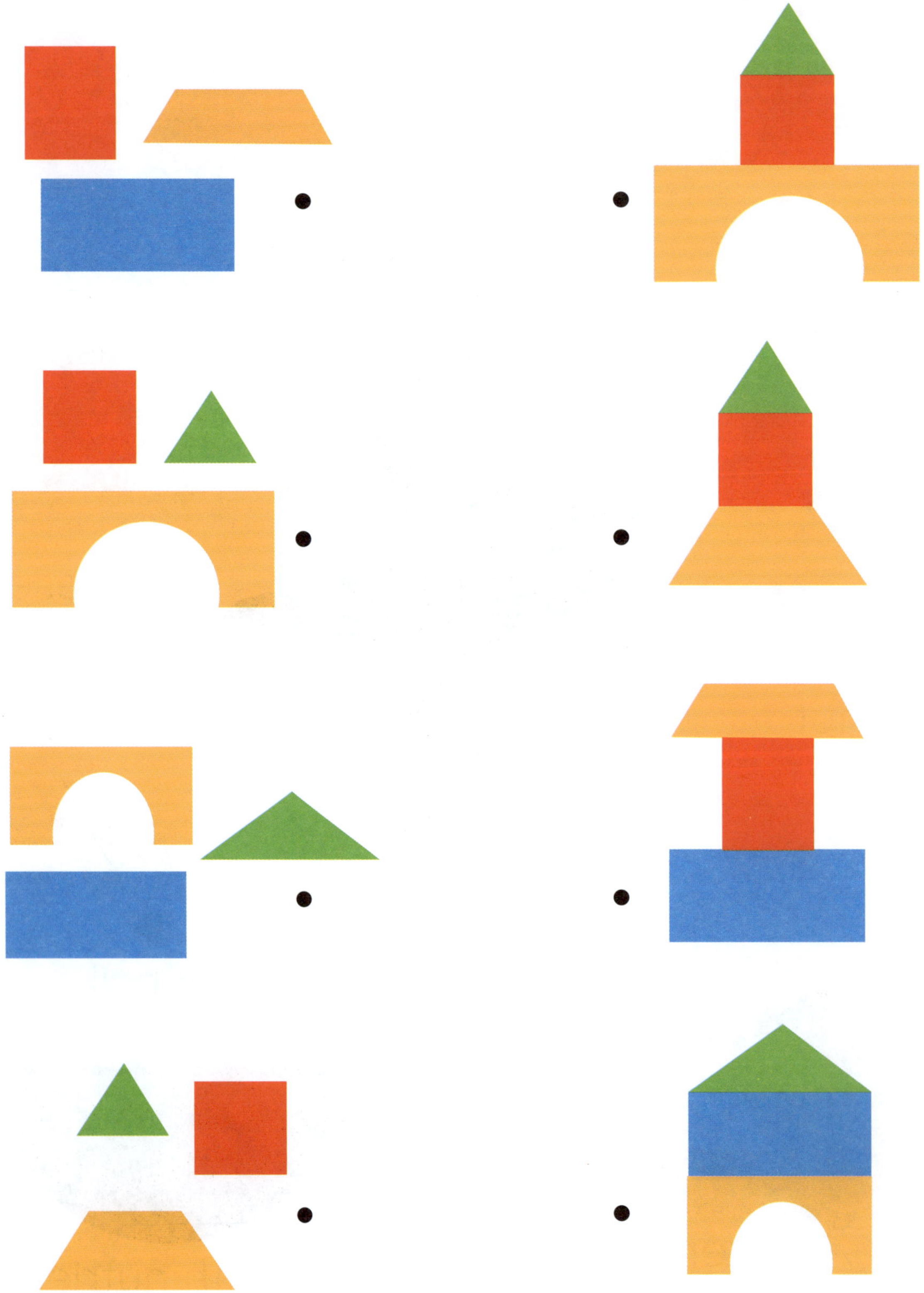

Count and circle the number names

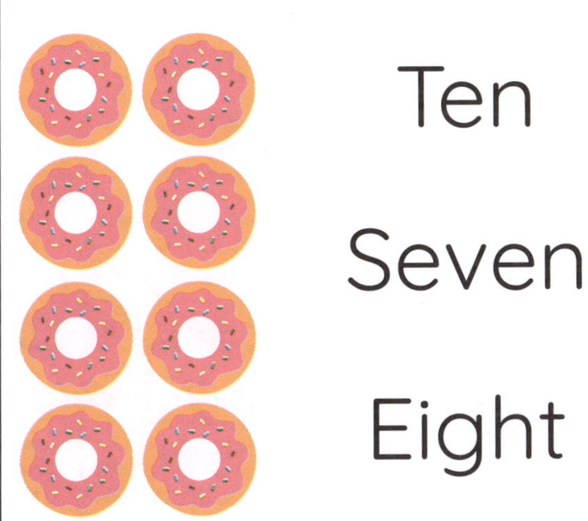

Ten

Seven

Eight

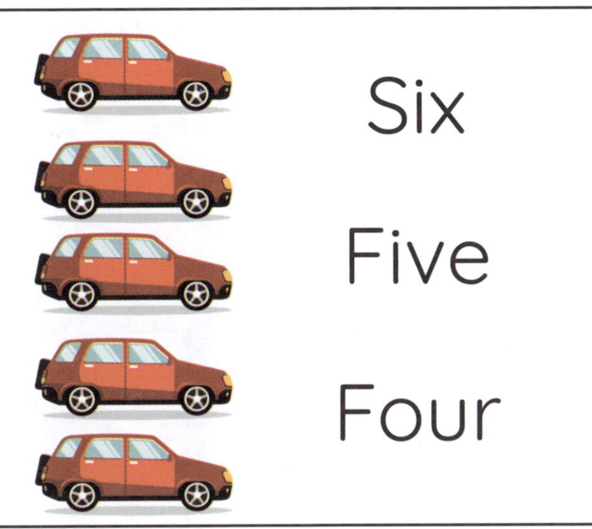

Six

Five

Four

Two

Four

Three

Three

Four

Two

Two

One

Three

Three

Four

Five

Fill in the missing numbers

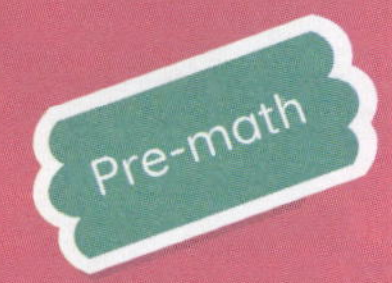

Tick the lighter object in each box

Merge the vowel and consonant to create two-letter words

e

Consonant	Word
b	eb
c	
d	
f	
g	
j	
k	
l	
m	
n	
p	
s	
t	

"e" sound words

-eb

web

-ed

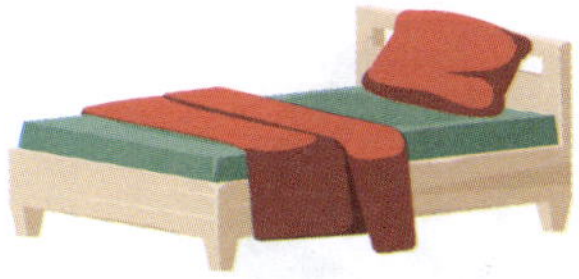

red bed fed led wed

-en

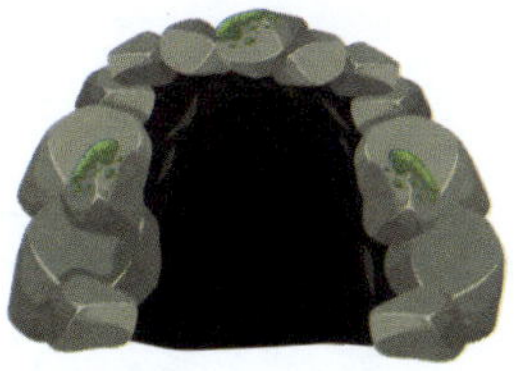

hen men pen ten den

-et

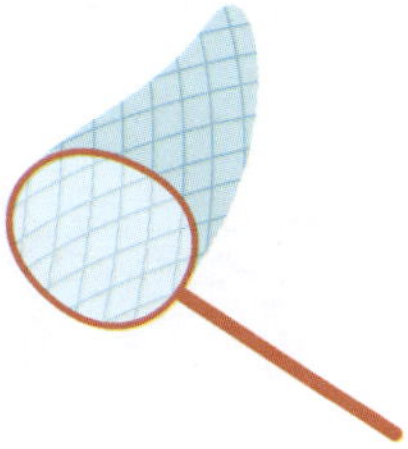

bet get jet let set

wet met net pet yet vet

-eg

beg leg keg

peg

Unscramble the "-ed" words and write them

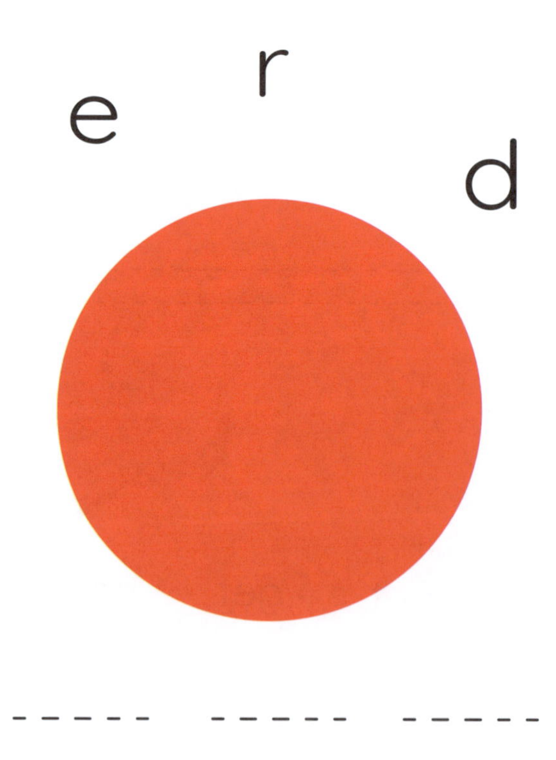

Search the words in the puzzle given below

peg beg keg leg meg

seg neg veg teg

h	v	p	e	l	m	s	t	z	e
q	e	k	e	g	d	e	c	b	g
t	g	k	q	u	i	k	g	q	r
m	n	t	s	e	t	v	q	y	q
g	m	b	q	v	n	e	g	n	l
s	n	q	e	q	b	u	s	h	e
a	r	b	a	g	d	a	a	c	g
g	y	g	e	d	g	b	e	q	e
u	t	e	g	e	h	j	g	u	n
s	q	i	p	s	e	g	u	e	e

Literacy

Read and fill in the blanks given below

A hen in the pen.

Hi! My name is Ben. I saw a hen in the pen. The hen laid ten eggs. Two men came to take the hen. They took the hen out of the pen and hid it in a den as they didn't want to give a yen.

ten men yen den Ben hen pen

A_______ in the _______ .

My name is _______

I saw a _______ in the _______.

The _______ laid ten eggs.

Two _______ came to take the hen.

Form words using the letters from the grid.

w	v	e	p
t	e	t	n
e	t	t	j

Tick the food that each animal eats

EVS

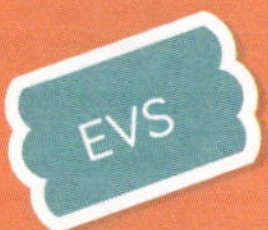

Circle the children helping in keeping the surrounding clean

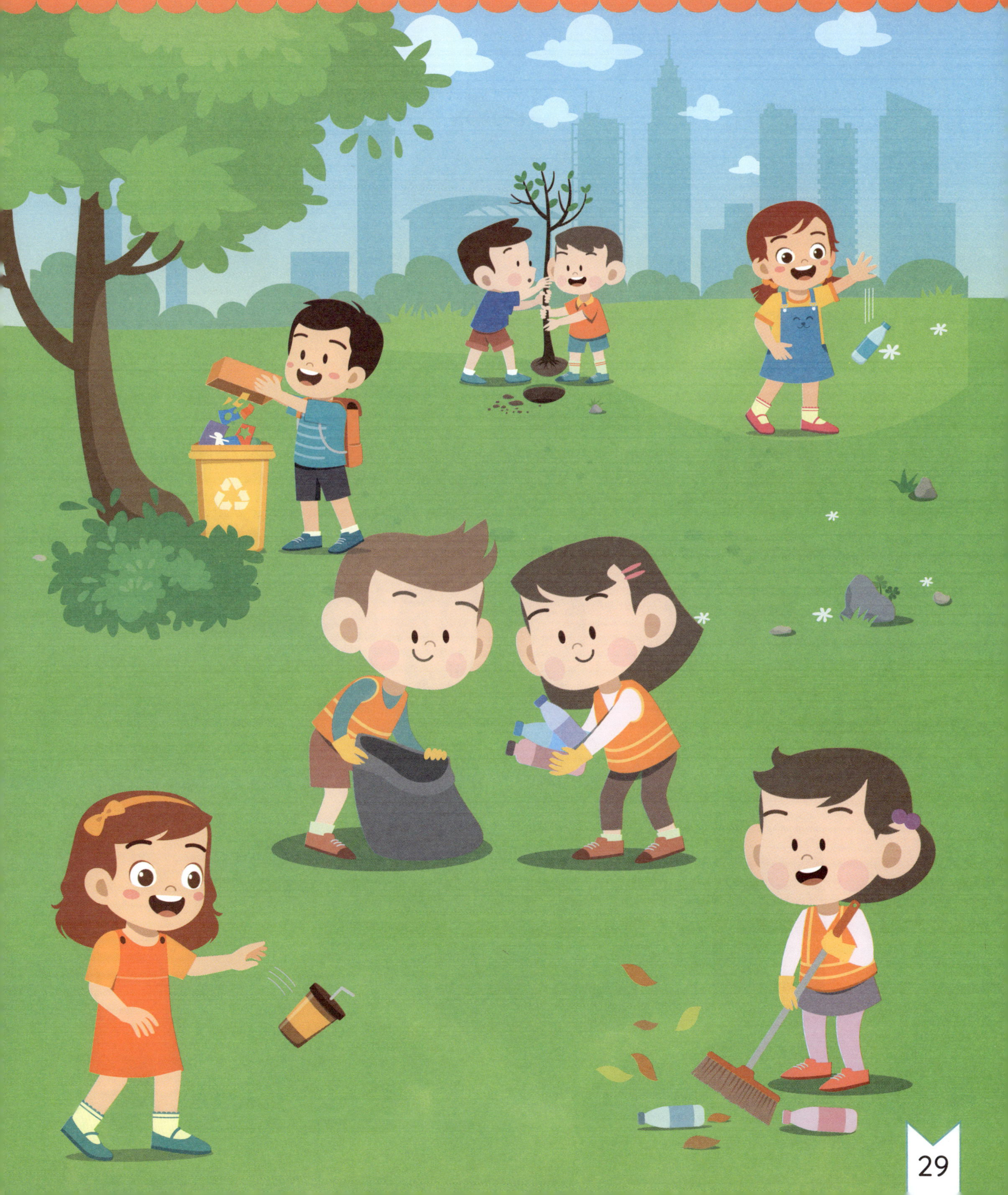

Match the pictures to where they belong

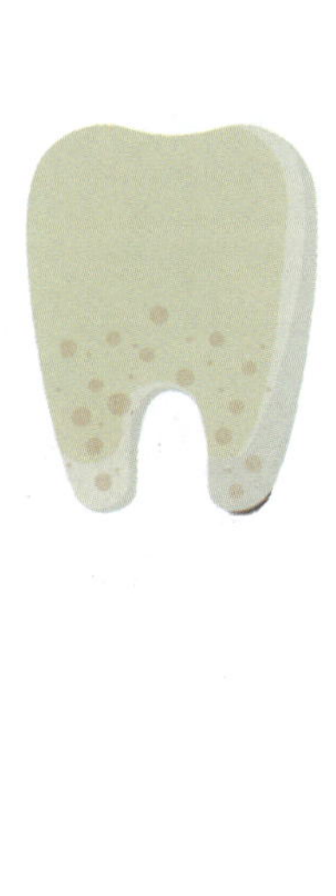

dirty

clean

EVS

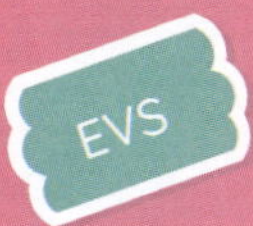

Write L for land, W for water and A for air transport

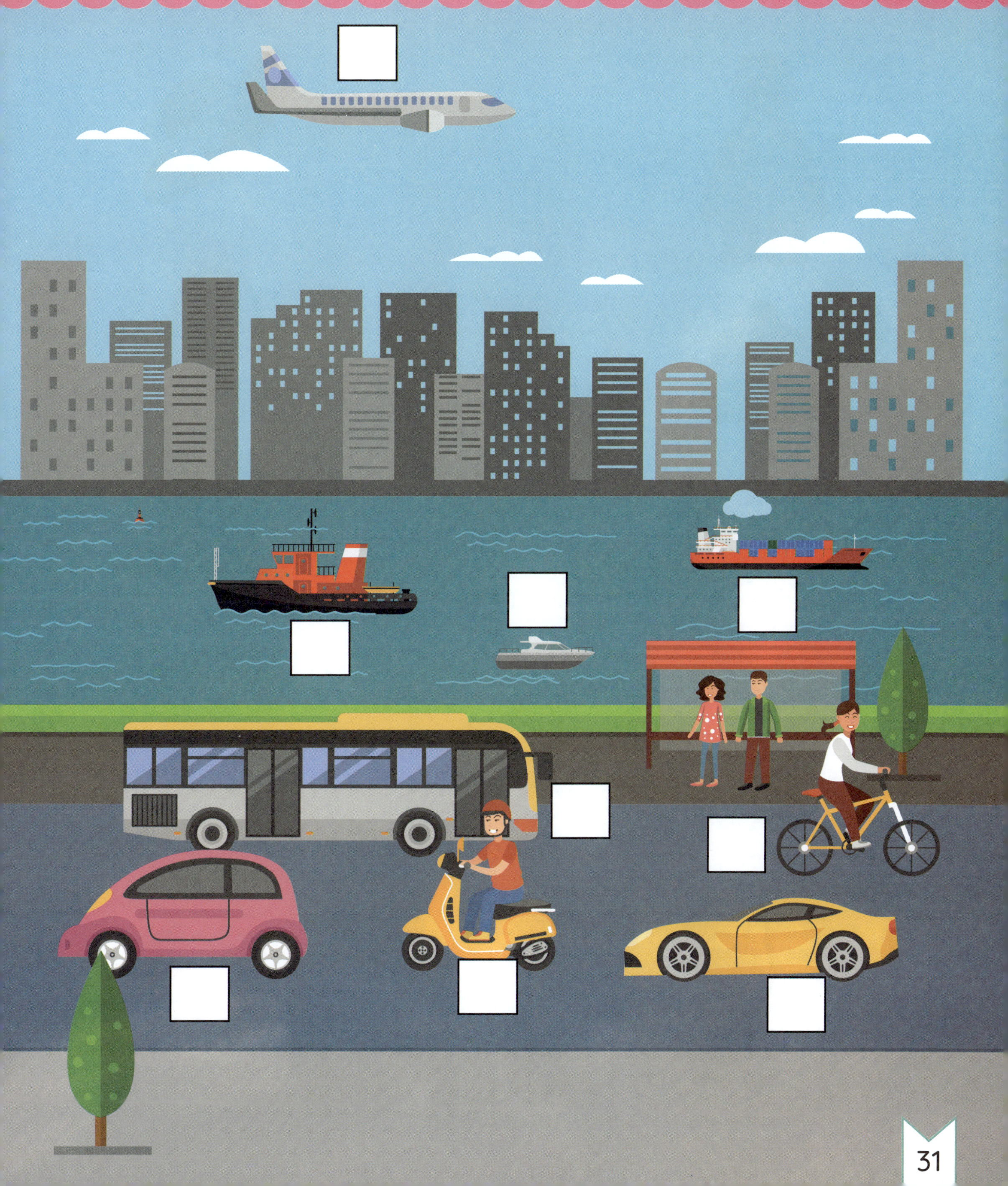

Match the pictures according to the seasons

MONSOON

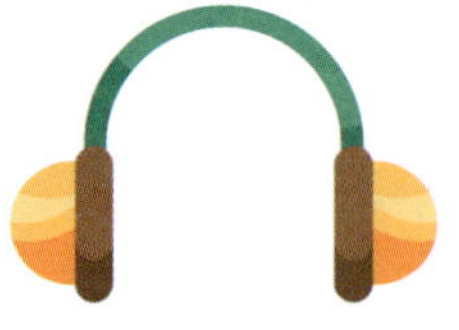

SUMMER

WINTER

Circle all living things

Circle all the non-living things

Pre-Math

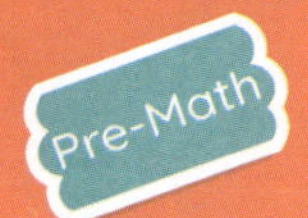

Circle the objects that are down

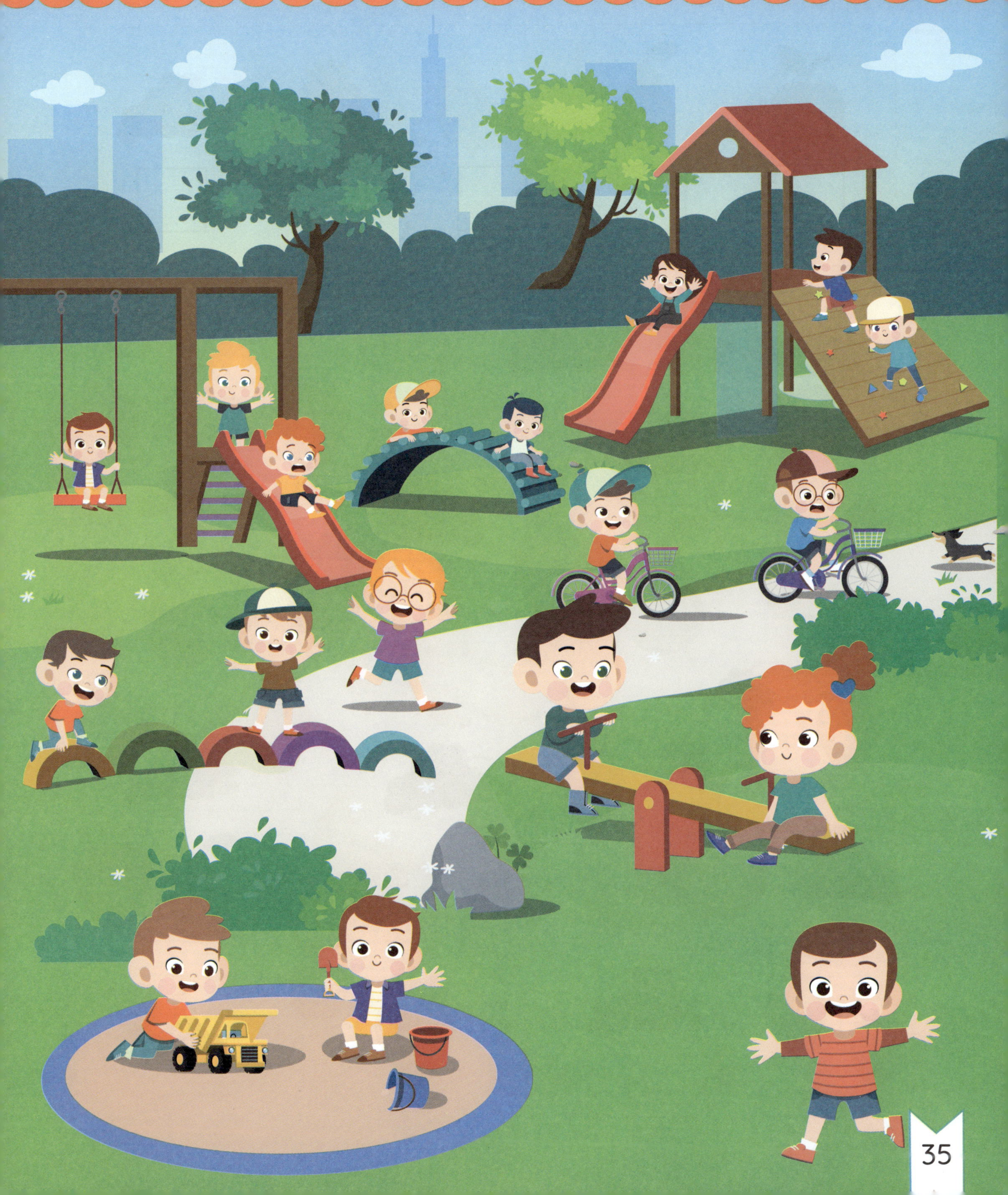

Numeracy

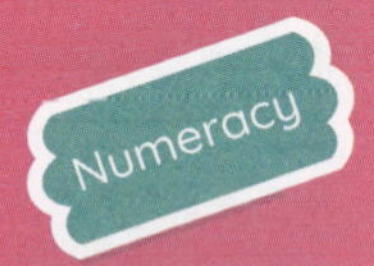

Count and write the number of fruits

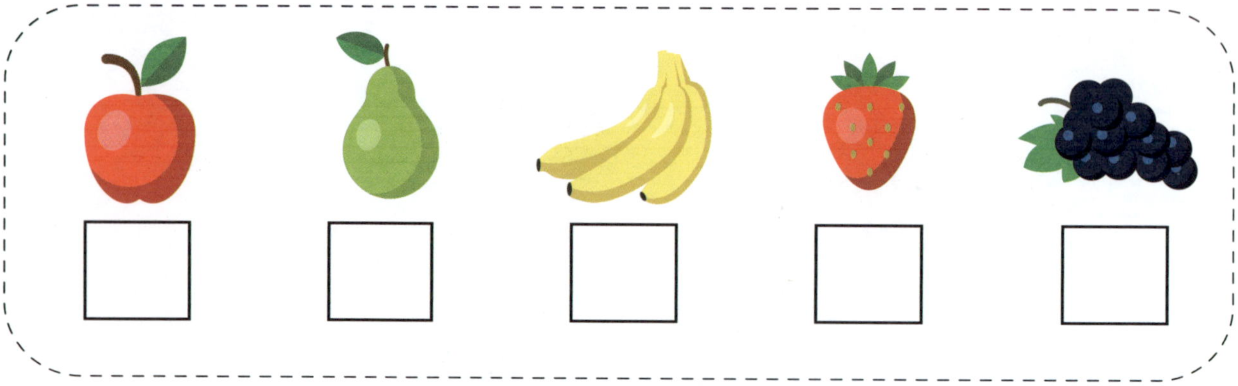

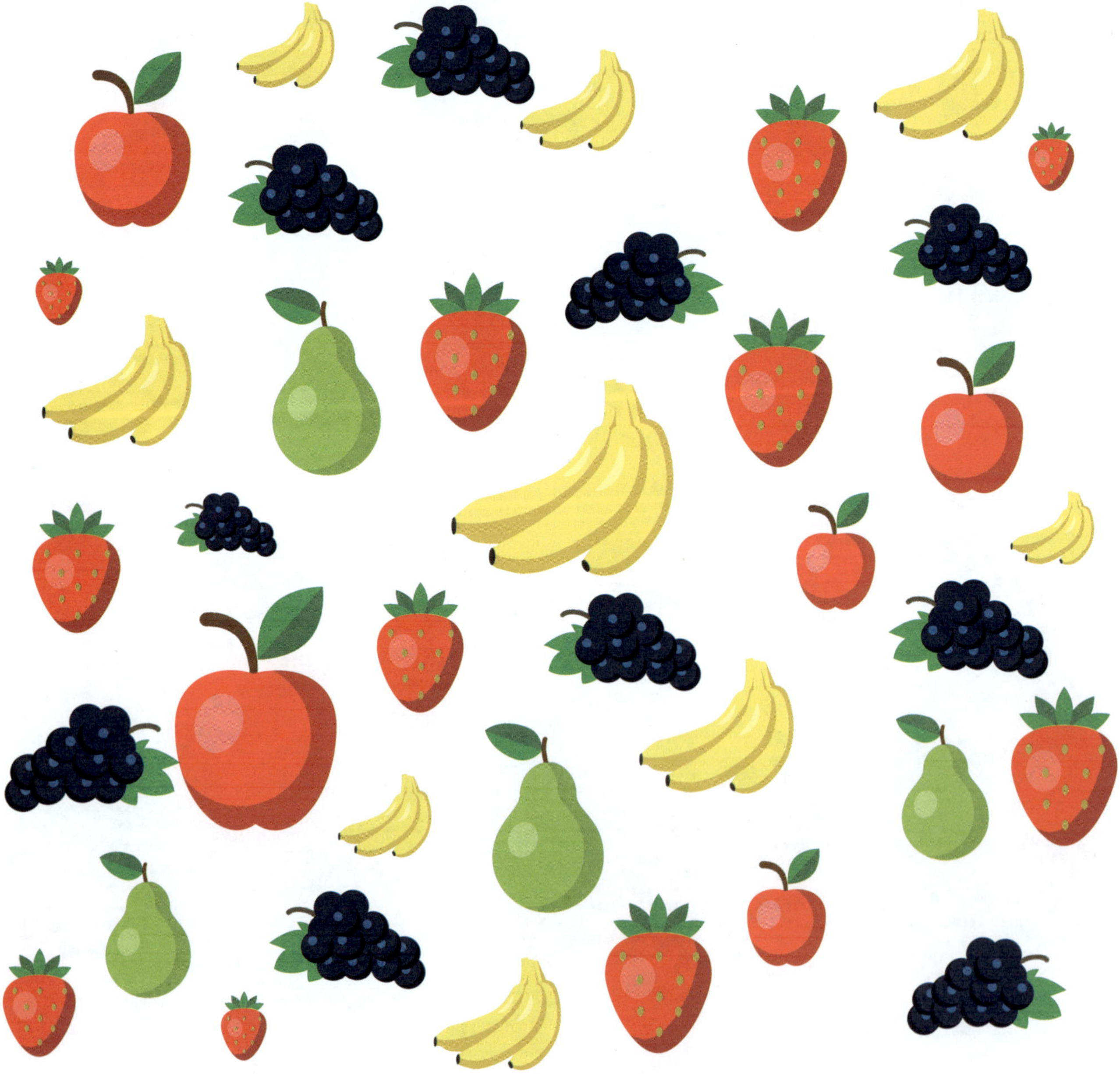

Tick the good habits

Count and match with the correct numbers

13 • • 

14 • • 

10 • • 

12 • • 

11 • • 

EVS

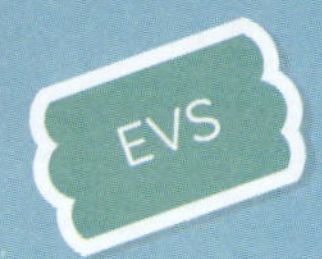

Circle only the fruits that have white seeds

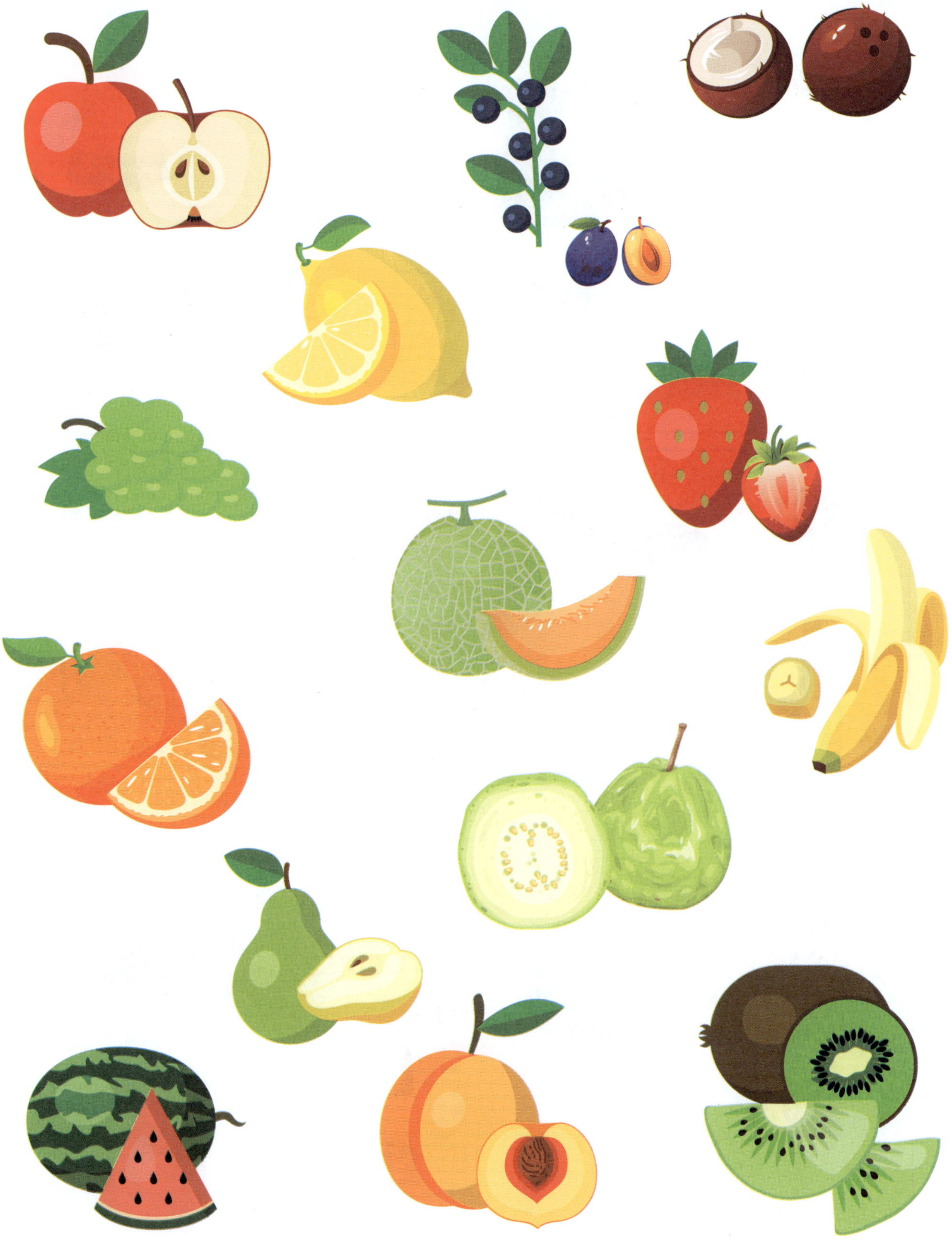

Circle the odd objects in each group

Circle the group that has less objects

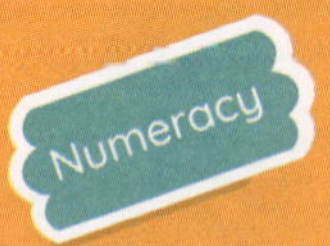

5 3	16 41
4 7	24 14
8 10	39 12
1 2	50 47

Numeracy

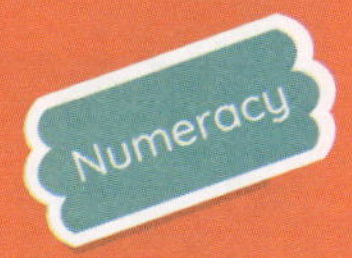

Count and write the number of each coloured safety pin

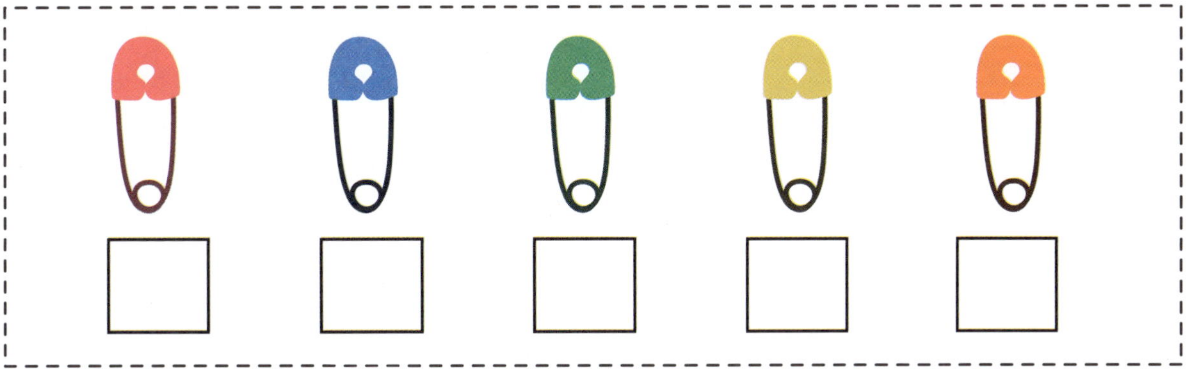

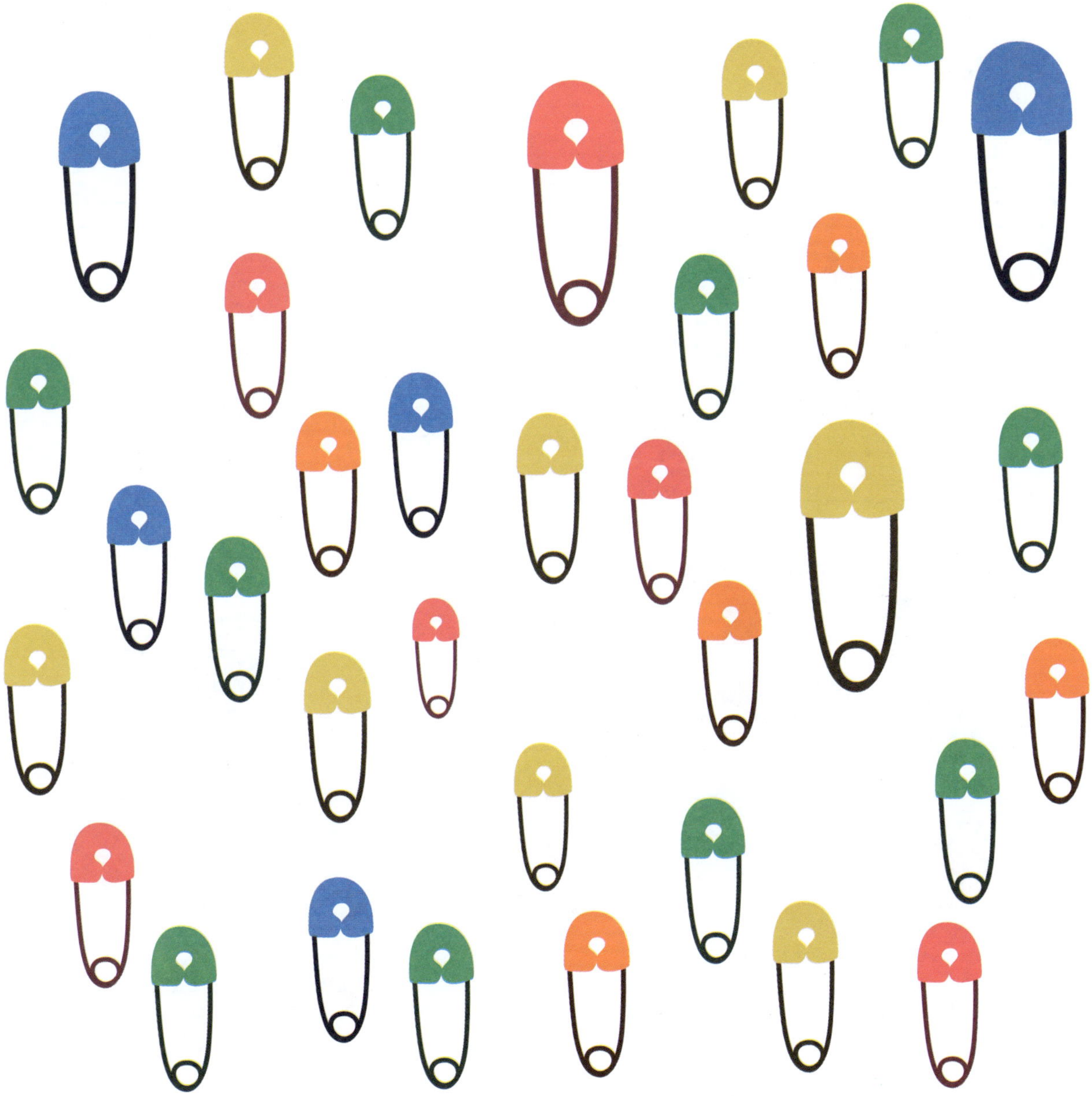

Circle the group that has more objects

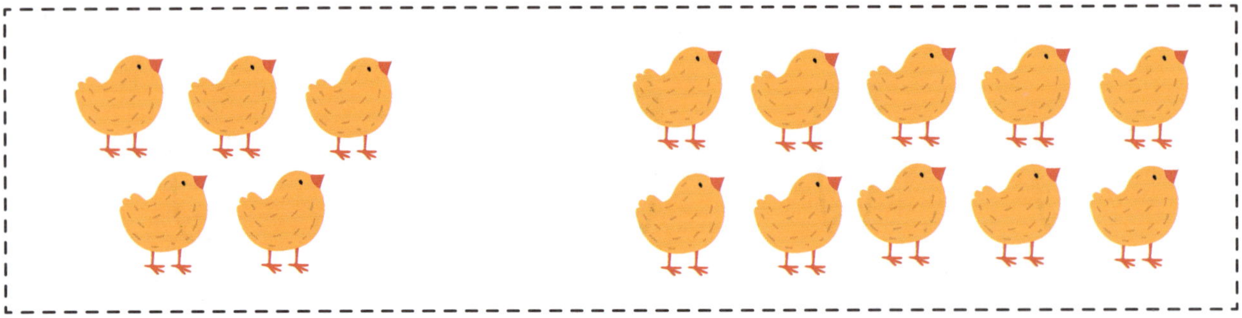

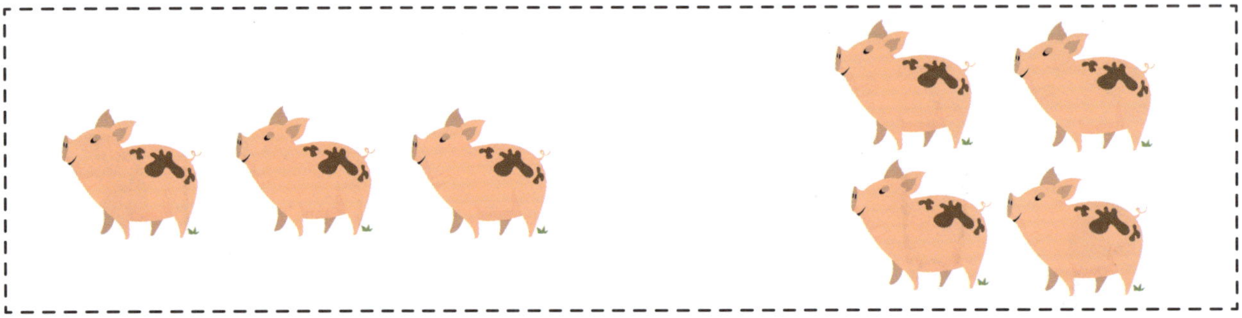

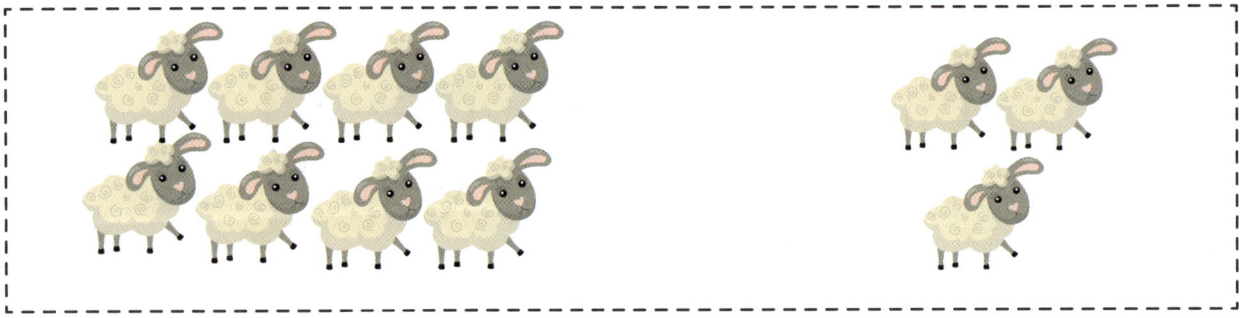

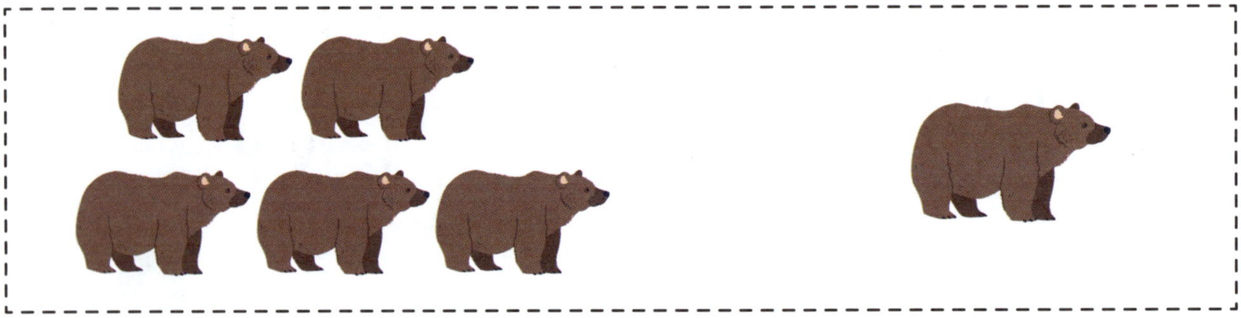

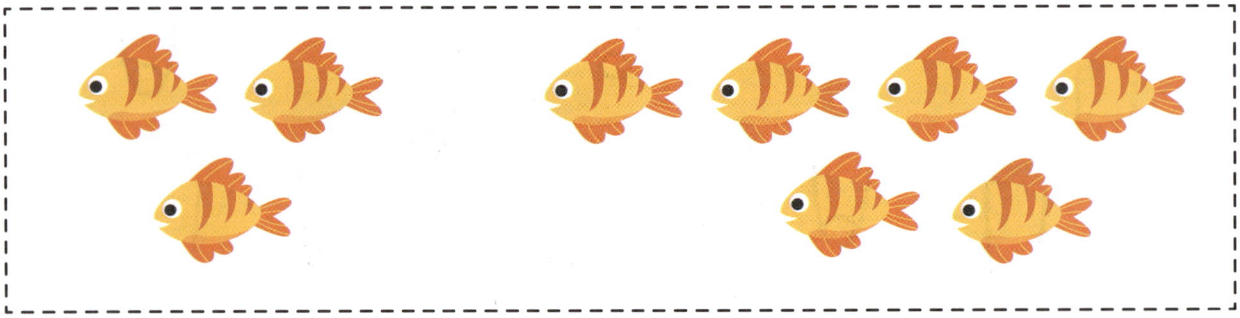

Merge the vowel and consonant to create two-letter words

i

b ib

c

d

f

g

j

k

l

m

n

p

s

t

x

"i" sound words

-ib

nib bib fib
rib

-it

sit fit lit hit
pit bit wit kit

-ix

mix fix six

-id

bid did hid
kid lid mid
rid

-ig

big dig fig
jig pig wig

-in

fin bin pin
tin win

-ip

dip hip lip
nip pip rip
sip tip zip

-im

dim vim
him rim

Read the passage and fill in the correct answer below.

The pig

A pig had a wig.
The wig was big.
The pig went to a gig.
The pig did a jig.
The pig ran in the park and fell in the big pit.

Fill in the blanks
(wig, gig, big, pig)

1. A pig had a __________.
2. The pig went to a __________.
3. The ______ did a jig.
4. The pig ran in the park and fell in the __________ pit.

Literacy

Identify and colour the words with "-id" only

kid
lid
den
big
ten
did
get
yet
pig
mid
pet
met
net
hen
hid
yen
bid
rid
pen

Connect words to pictures

bib •

• 

fib •

• 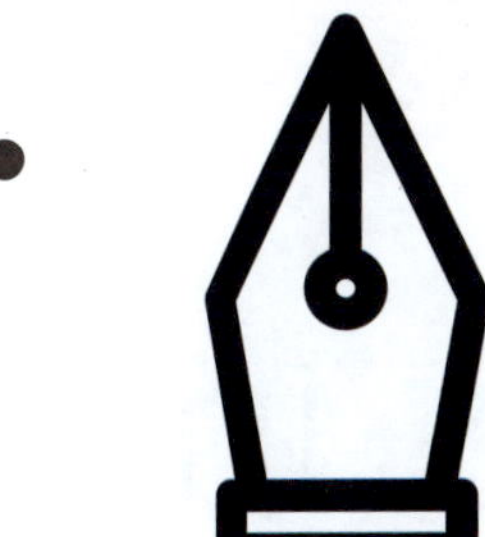

rib •

• 

nib •

• 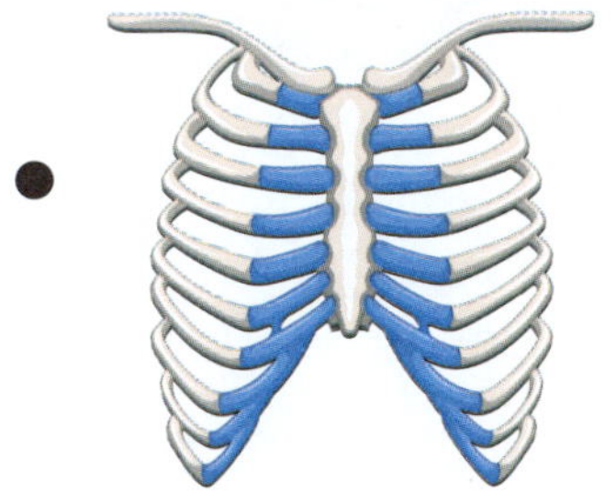

Complete the words using the missing letters

p t

_ _ in

_ _ in

_ _ in

_ _ in

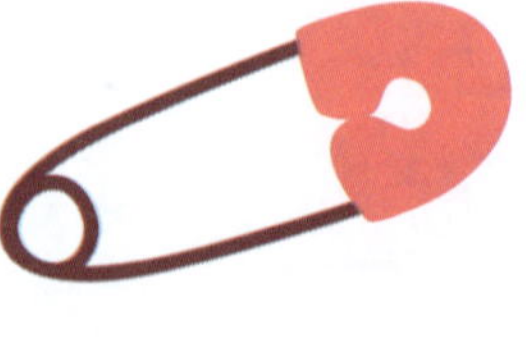

_ _ in

Trace the first letters and connect words to pictures

dim 

him 

rim 

vim 

Look at the pictures and complete the words

s t z l

_ _ ip

_ _ ip

_ _ ip

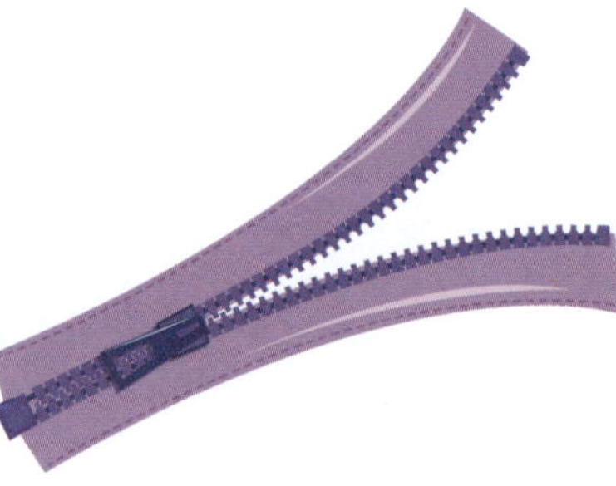

_ _ ip

_ _ ip

Spot words containing "-it"

h	e	f	i	t	d	k	i
i	a	l	a	e	k	i	i
t	h	p	i	t	a	t	r
s	i	t	f	l	i	t	s

Name the pictures

1. kit 2. sit 3. pit 4. fit 5. lit

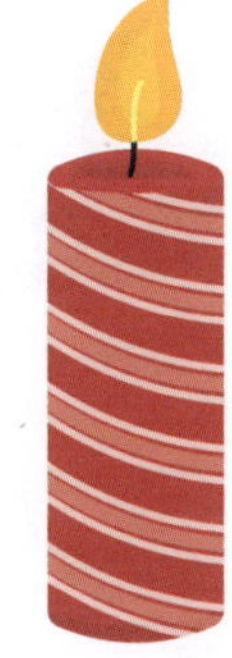

• six

• mix

• fix

Cognitive development

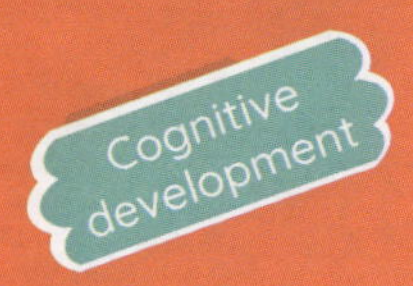

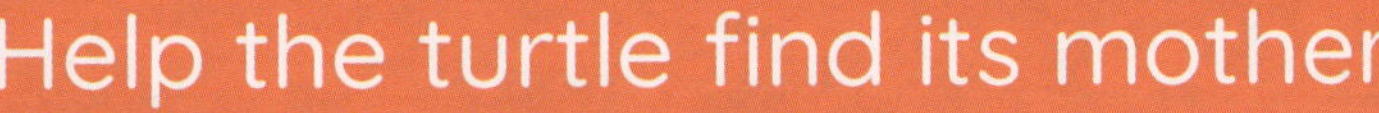

Help the turtle find its mother

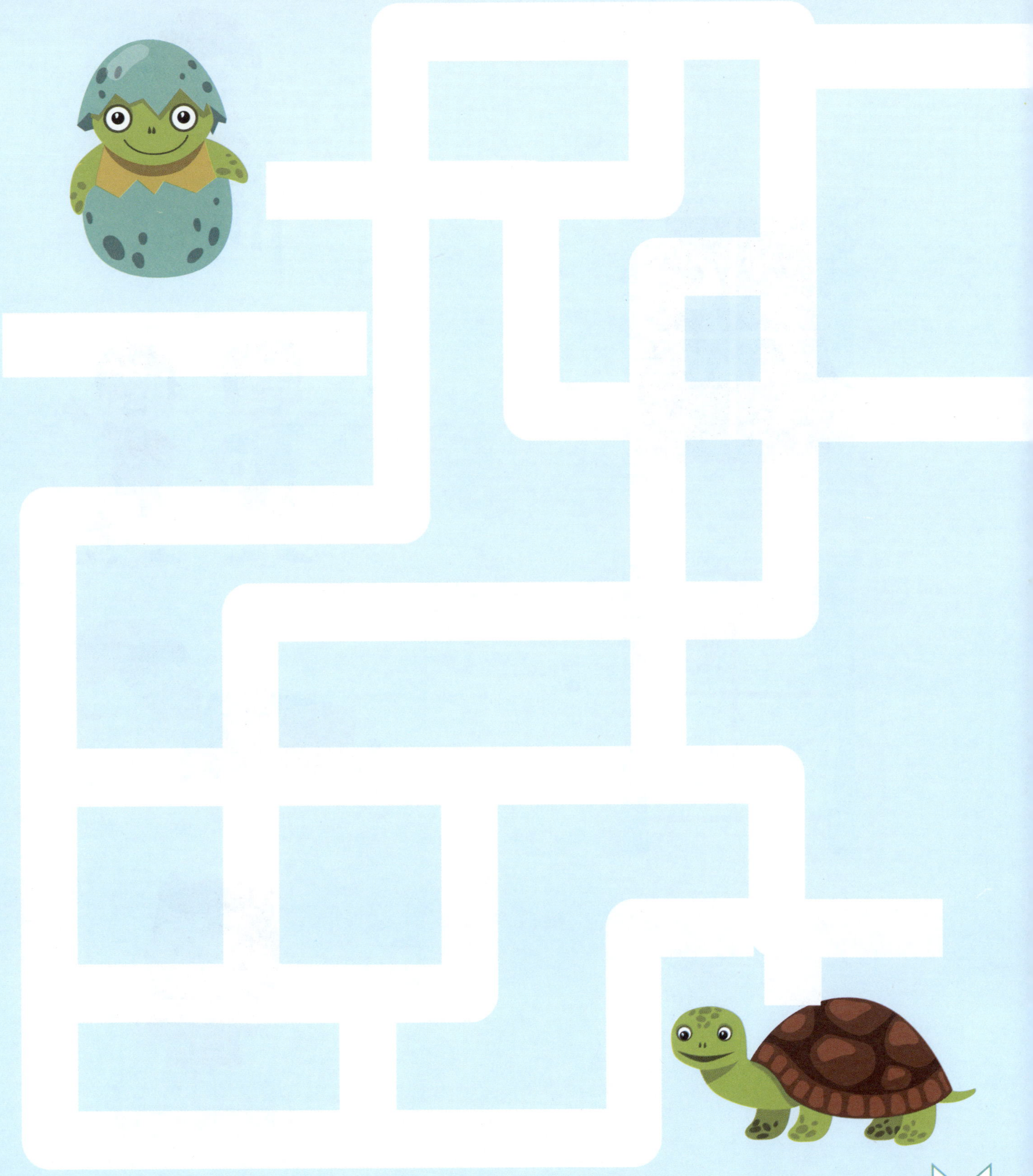

Match the day and night routines

Match the correct front and back images

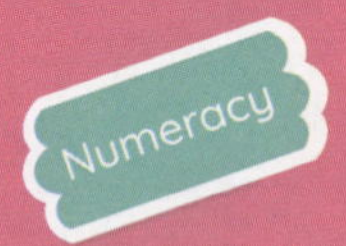

Arrange the numbers in ascending and descending order

Ascending Order	Descending Order
73 65 59 33 82	54 12 28 47 82

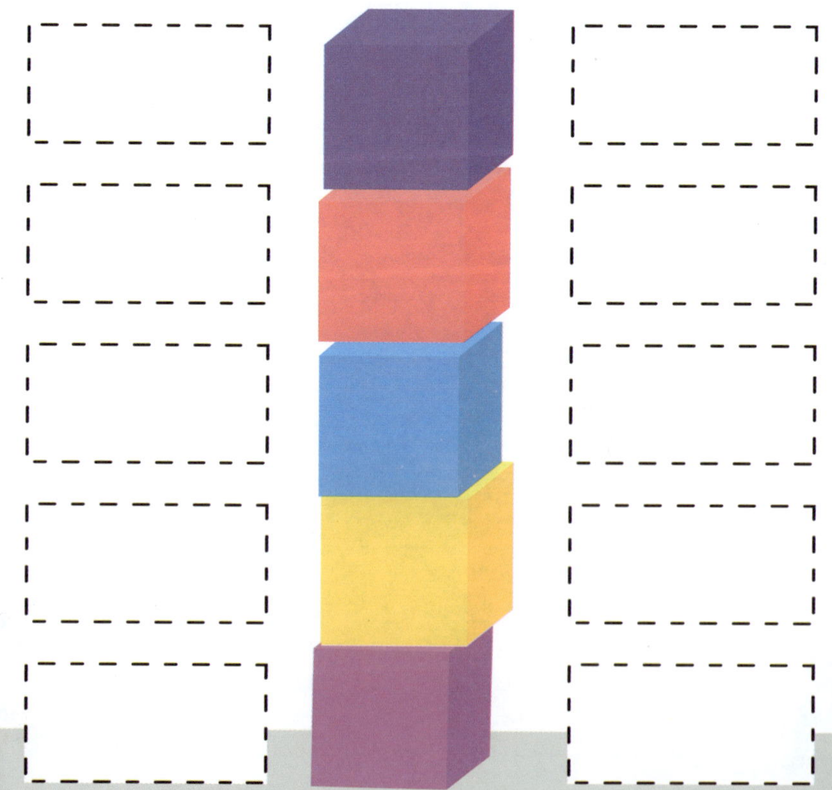

Cognitive development

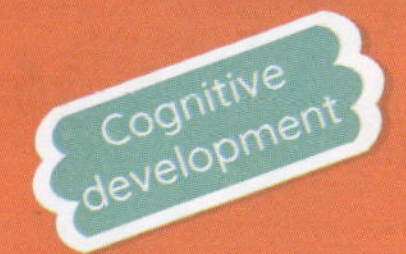

Match the musical instruments

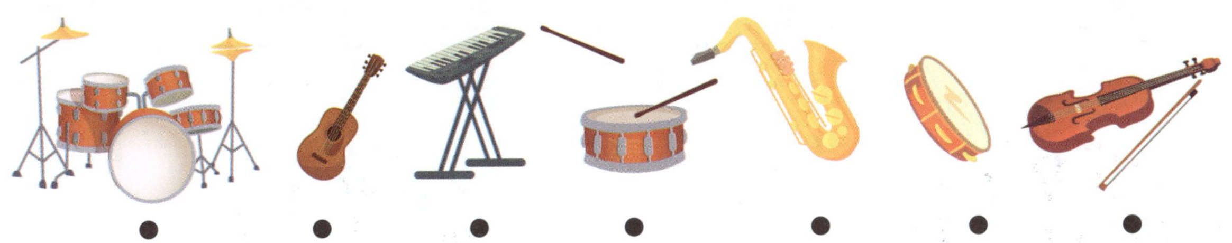

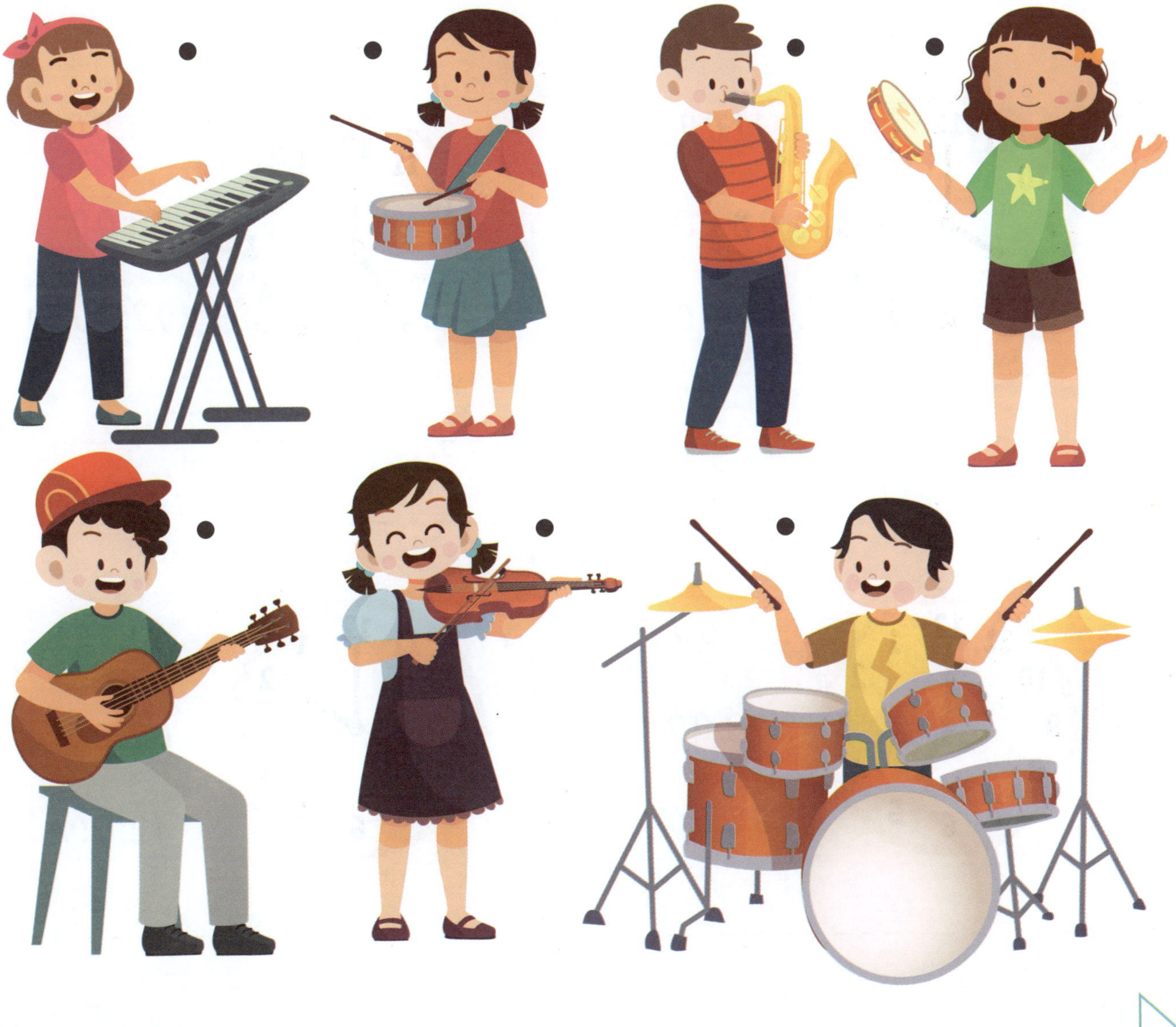

What is the time on the analogue clocks?

Count the number of objects and add them

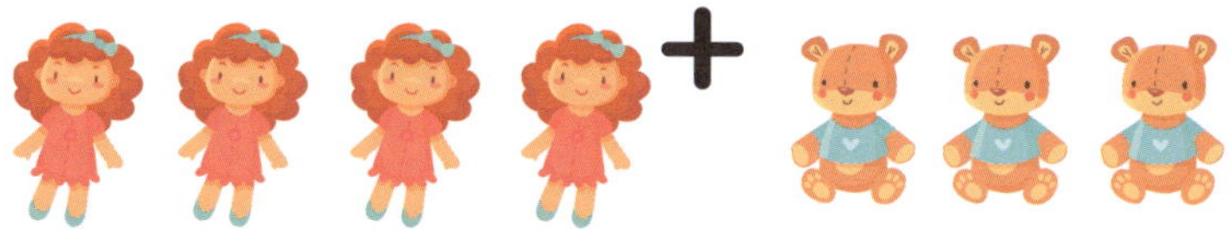

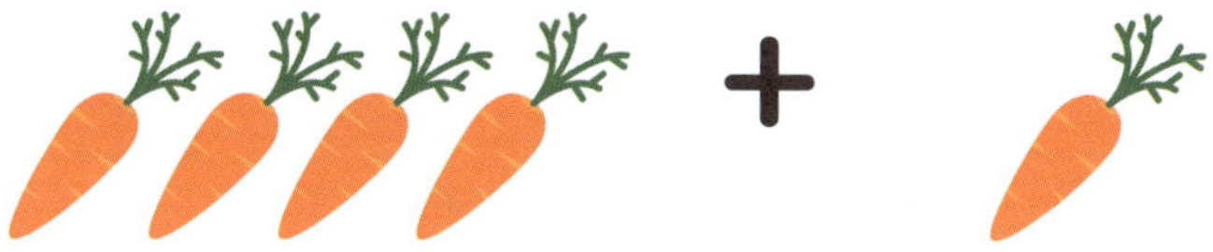

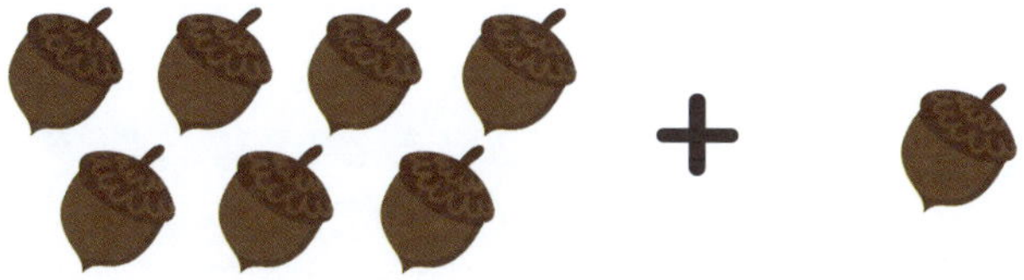

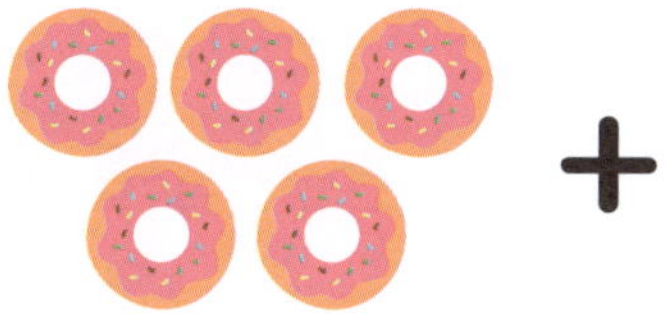

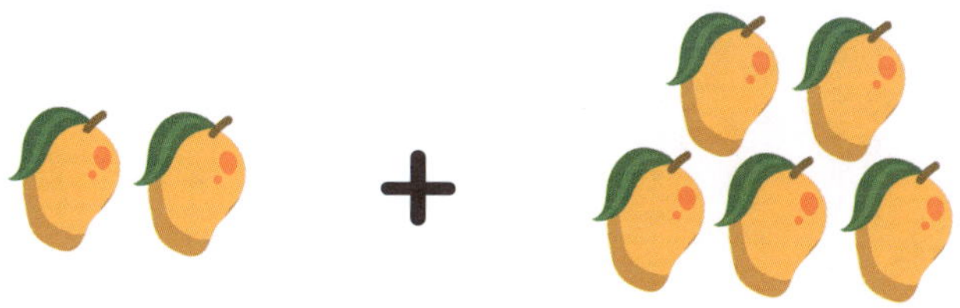

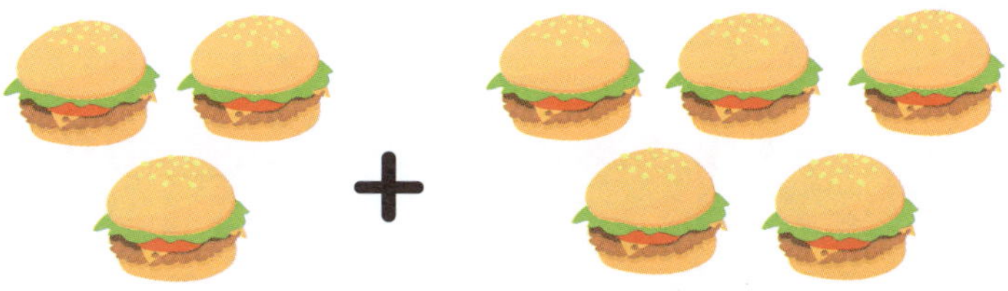

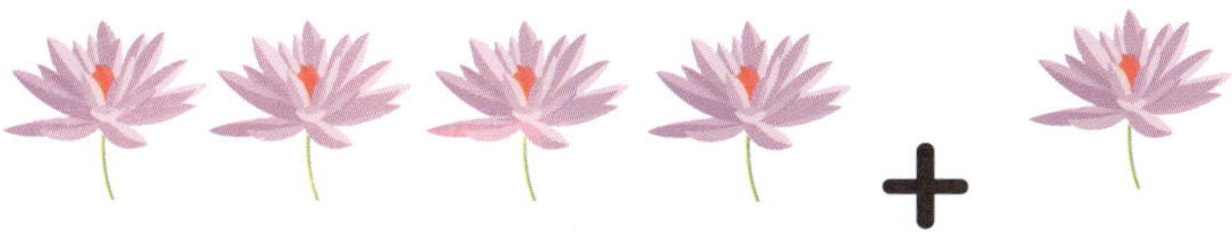

☐ + ☐ = ☐

☐ + ☐ = ☐

☐ + ☐ = ☐

☐ + ☐ = ☐

☐ + ☐ = ☐

☐ + ☐ = ☐

☐ + ☐ = ☐

Literacy

Merge the vowel and consonant to create two-letter words

o

b ____ob____

c ____________

d ____________

f ____________

g ____________

j ____________

k ____________

l ____________

m ____________

n ____________

p ____________

s ____________

t ____________

x ____________

Literacy

"o" sound words

-od

cod god pod
rod nod

-oy

boy toy

-og

dog hog fog
jog log

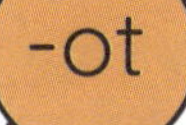

-ot

pot dot got hot
cot lot not jot rot

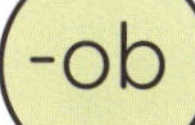

-ob

cob job
mob rob sob

-ox

fox box

-op

hop mop pop
top cop

Match the words to the pictures

cob •

• 

mob •

• 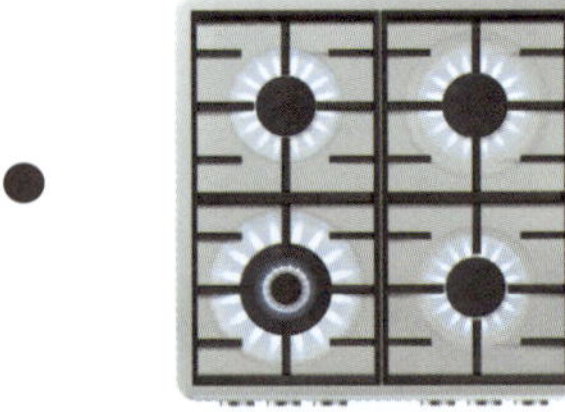

job •

• 

sob •

• 

rob •

• 

hob •

• 

Rob's Bot

Rob has a bot. He likes his bot a lot. He got the bot in the box. He did not get his bot in a pot. The bot is not hot. The bot cannot run. The bot has a dot. Rob likes his bot a lot.

Rob has a ____________________

- bot
- dog
- pig

Rob got the bot in a ____________________

- pit
- pot
- box

Rob likes his bot a ____________________

- bit
- lot
- ten

Trace the first letters and connect the words to the pictures

sod •

cod •

nod •

pod •

rod •

Write the correct words

top	hop	cop	mop	pop	stop

I use a __________ to clean

I like to __________ in the air!

I can ask the __________ for help.

The popcorn goes __________

STOP __________ at the end of the road.

The man climbs to the  __________

Look at the picture and write the beginning letter to complete the word

____og

____og

____og

____og

____og

Literacy

Match the empty objects to the empty glass and full objects to the full glass

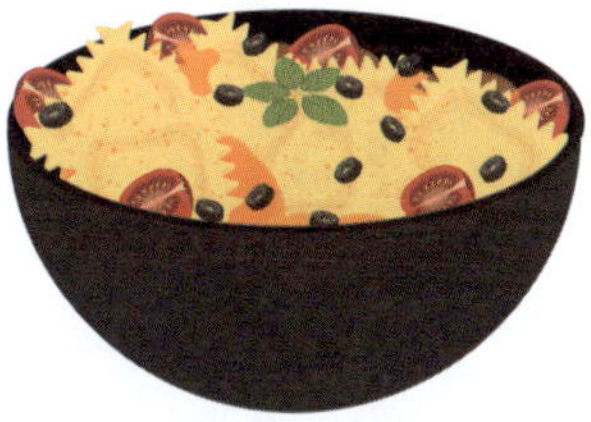

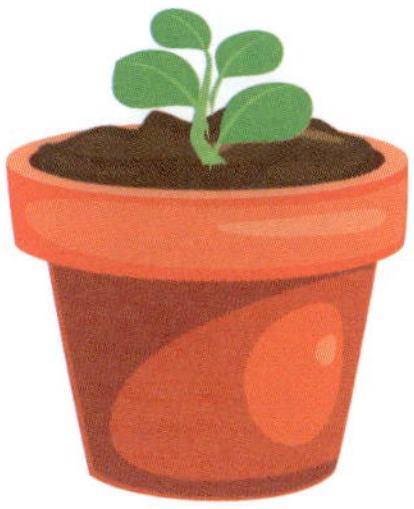

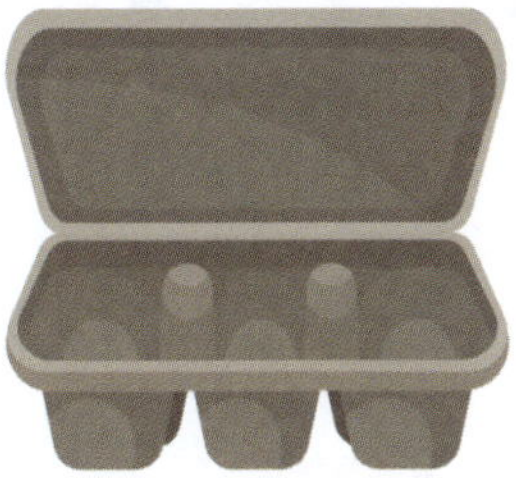

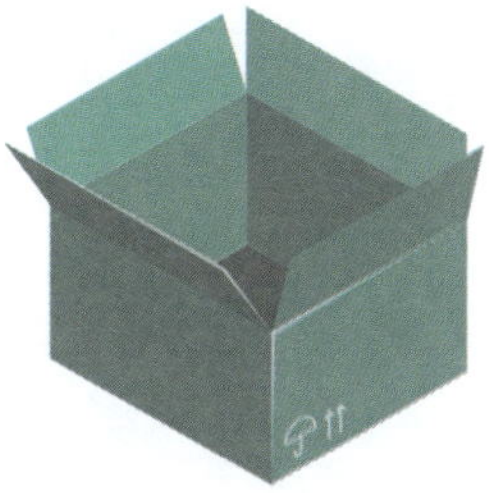

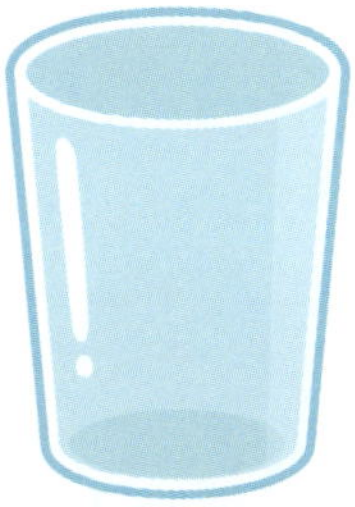

empty

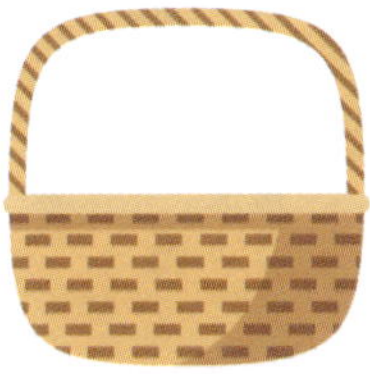

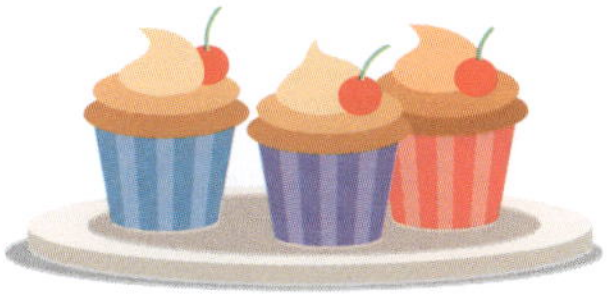

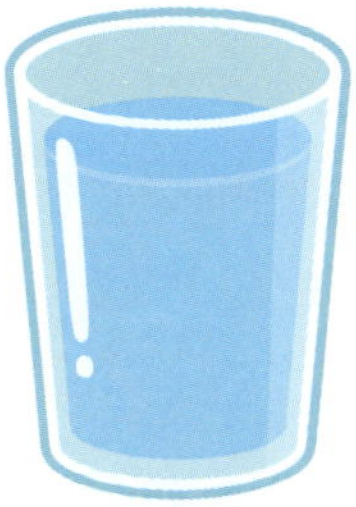

Full

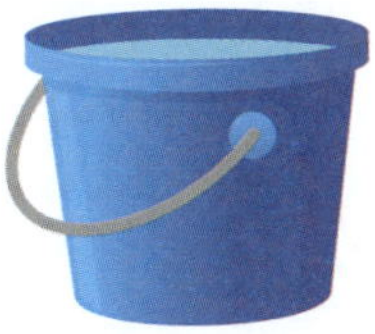

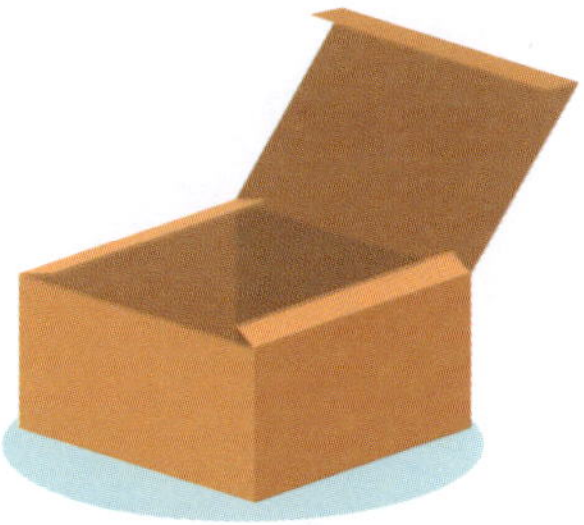

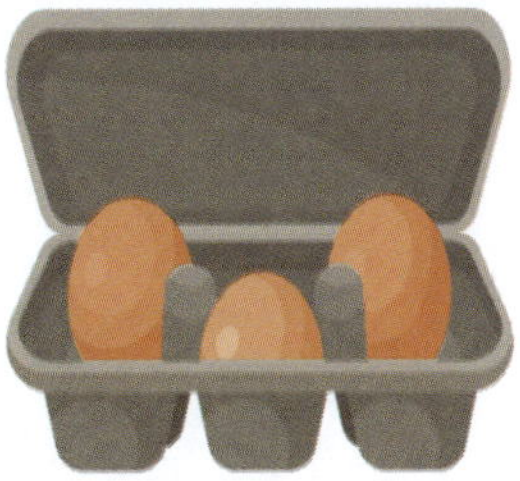

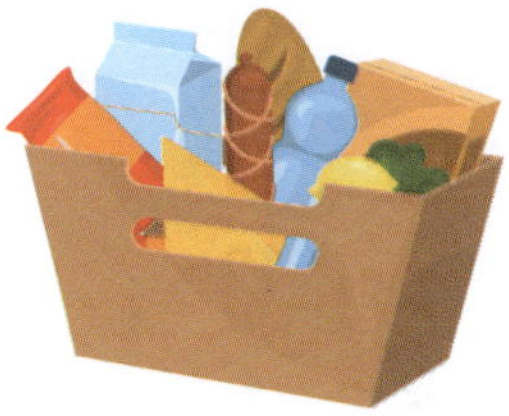

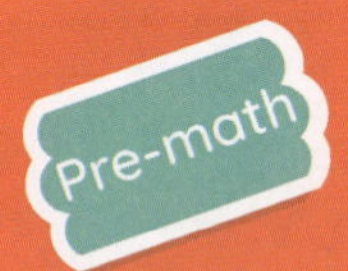

Read the time and match

• 12:00

• 06:00

• 01:00

• 05:00

• 03:00

Match these animals to their appropriate habitats

Tick the odd one out

Tick the healthy food item and cross the unhealthy food item

POP CORN

Numeracy

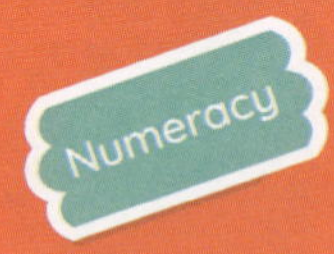

Count the corners of each shape and circle the correct answer

1	0	2

2	3	4

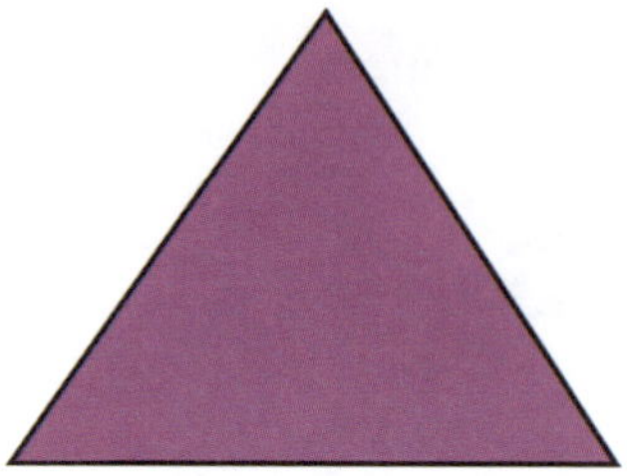

3	1	2

4	2	5

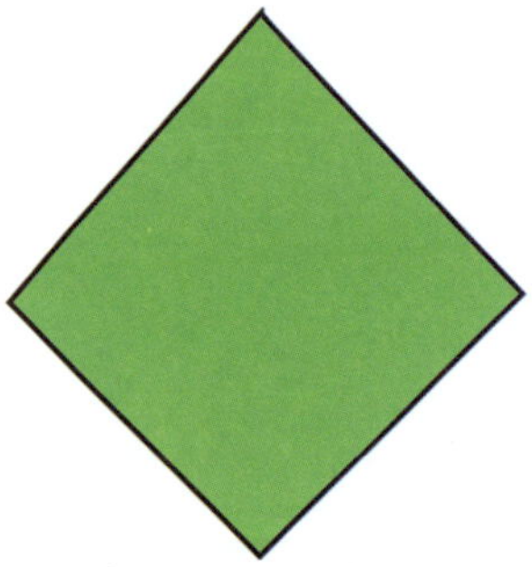

2	5	4

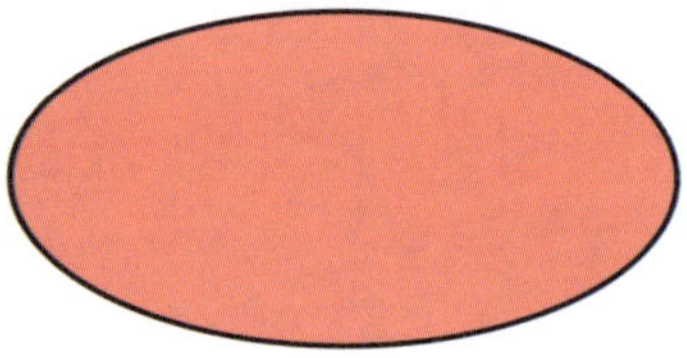

0	1	2

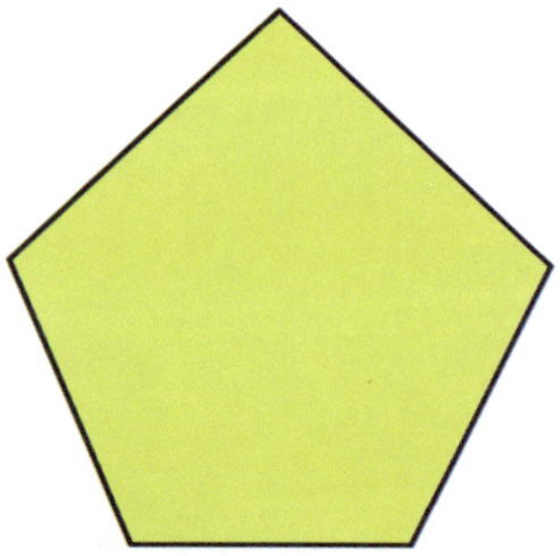

6	5	4

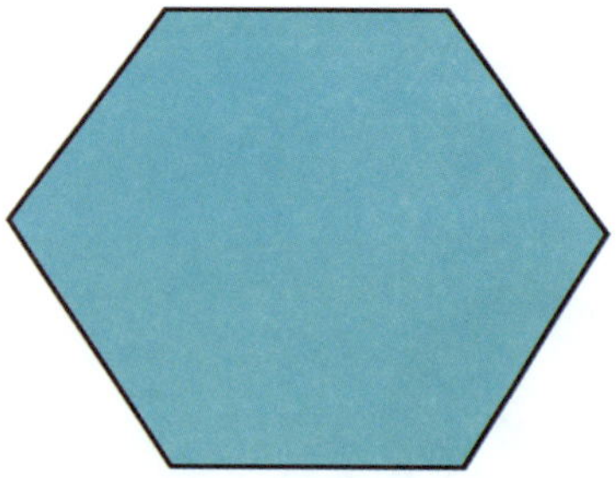

9	8	6

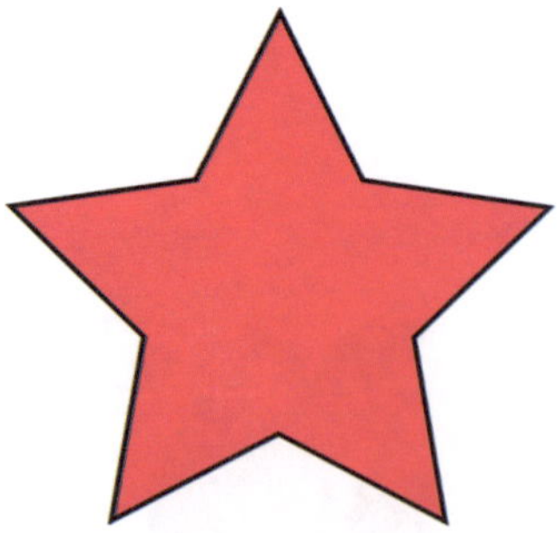

8	5	6

Add the objects in each row

+ =

+ =

+ =

+ =

+ =

Literacy

Merge the vowel and consonant to create two-letter words

u

b	ub
c	
d	
f	
g	
j	
k	
l	
m	
n	
p	
s	
t	
x	

"-ug" sound words

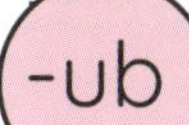

-ub

cub dub hub

rub sub tub

-ug

dug

hug bug rug

tug jug mug

-ut

hut nut

but cut

-un

sun fun gun nun bun run

-up

cup pup

sup

-um

gum mum

sum

-ud

bud mud

Trace the first letters and connect words to pictures

sub •

tub •

cub •

rub •

hub •

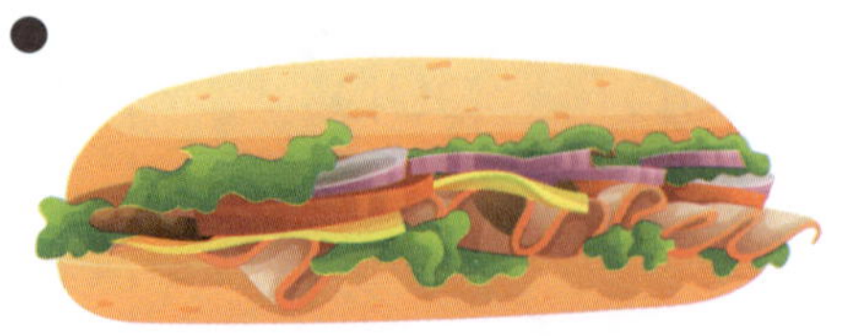

bug hug jug mug rug

tug dug

I can see a bug. The bug is near the  jug. The jug is on the

Tom drinks water from the 

mug. Pam dug the soi  plant seeds. Tom pours water

from the jug. Pam a  Tom

hug each other.

Unscramble the words and write

u n b

___ ___ ___

n s u

___ ___ ___

u r n

___ ___ ___

g n u

___ ___ ___

u n f

___ ___ ___

u n n

___ ___ ___

Write the begining letter and complete the word

___ut

___ut

___ut

EVS

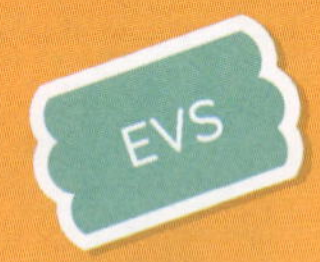

Find the objects that float or sink and match them to the right tub.

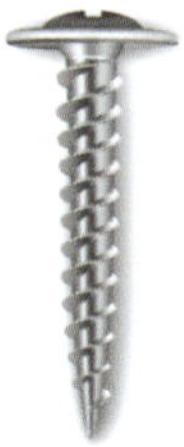

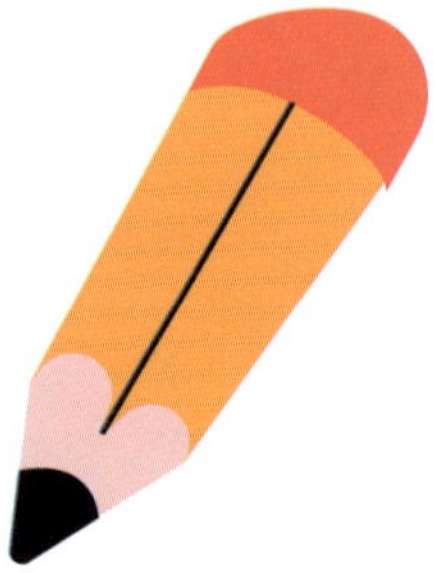

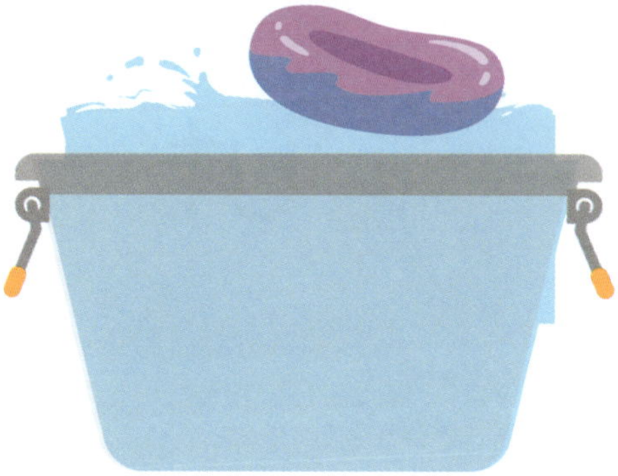

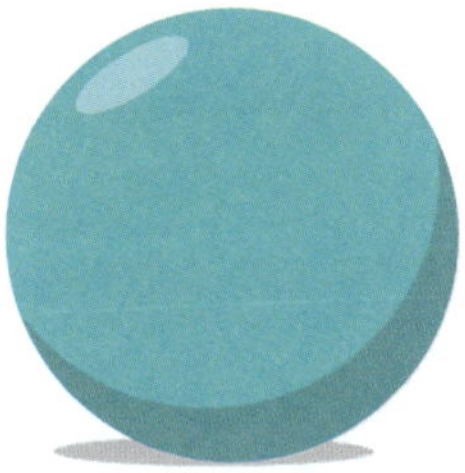

Float

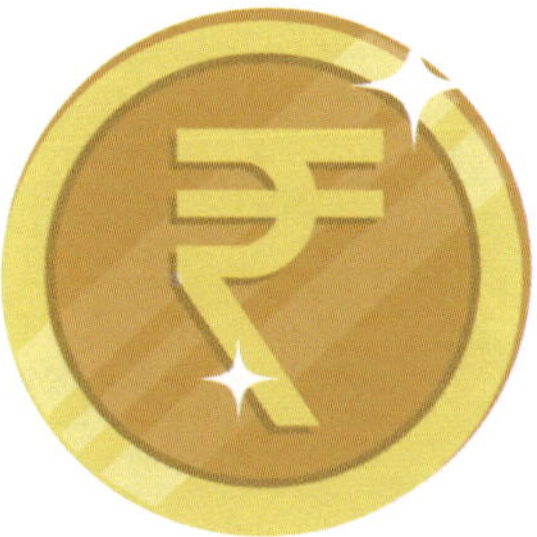

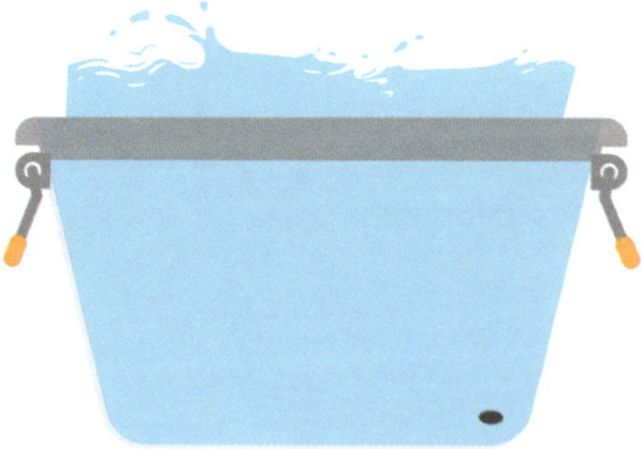

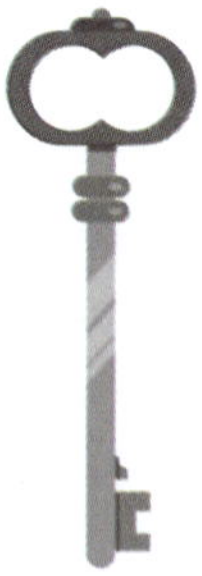

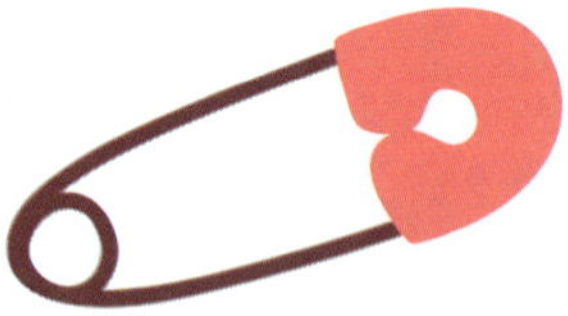

Sink

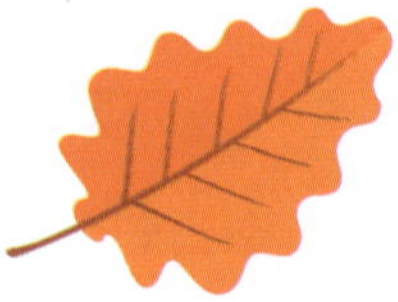

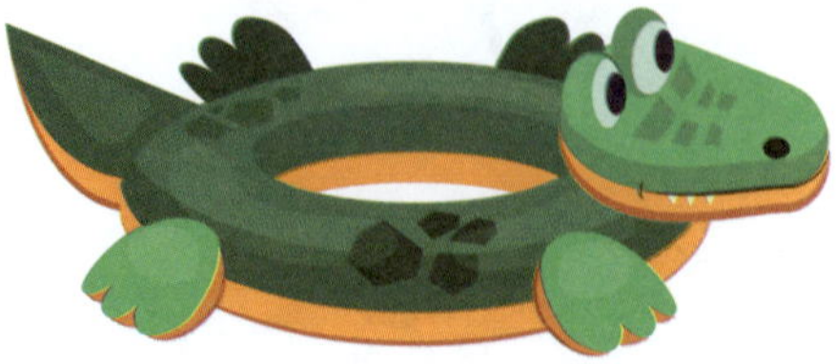

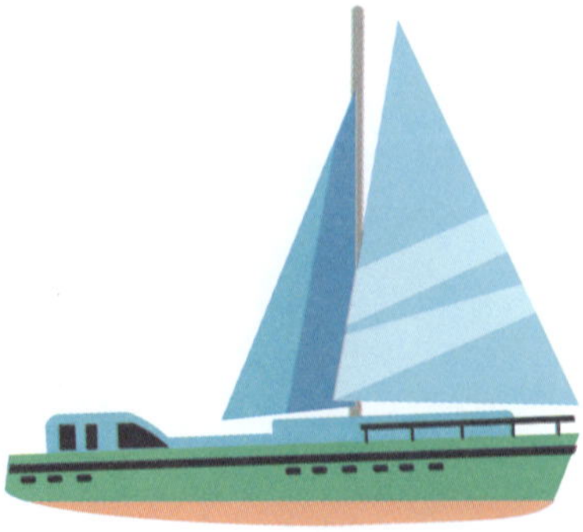

Circle the activities that need water

Where do they belong?

Good Manners

Bad Manners

Trace a circle around the habitat of each animal.

   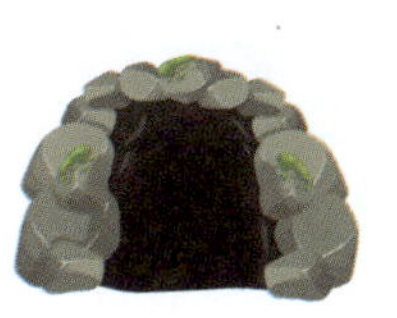

Match the currency notes with their values

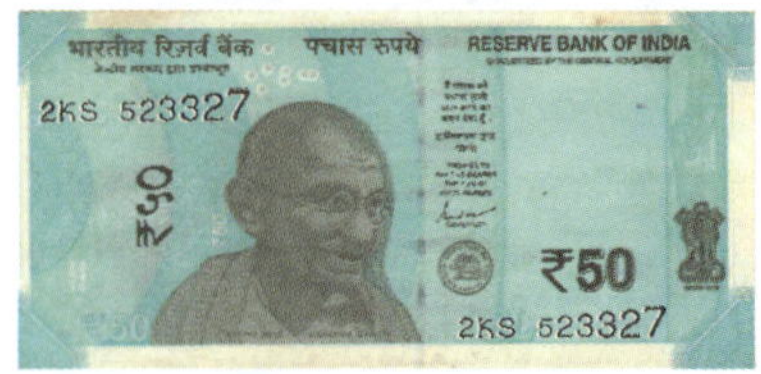	•	• ₹20
	•	• ₹100
	•	• ₹2000
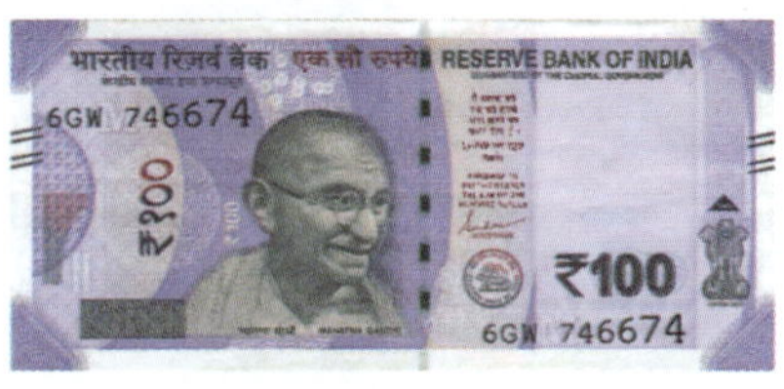	•	• ₹50
	•	• ₹500
	•	• ₹5
	•	• ₹10
	•	• ₹200

Do as directed

Tick only the taller objects

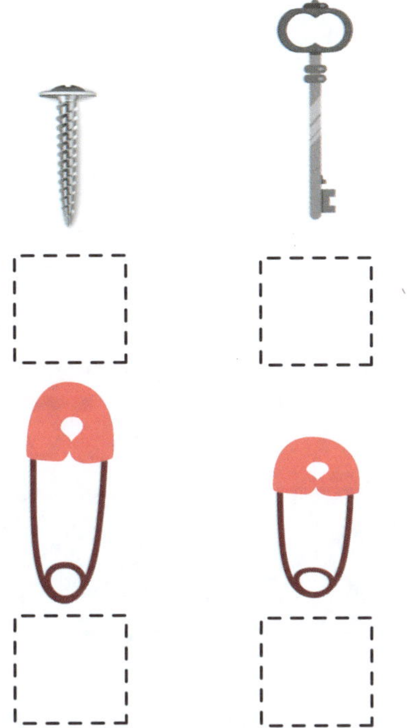

Tick only the shorter objects

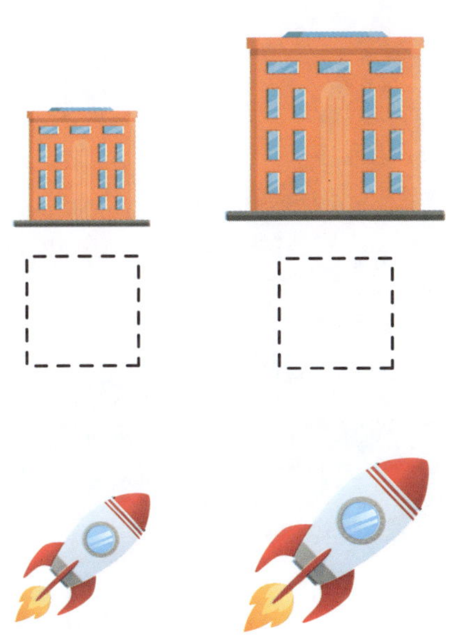

Numeracy

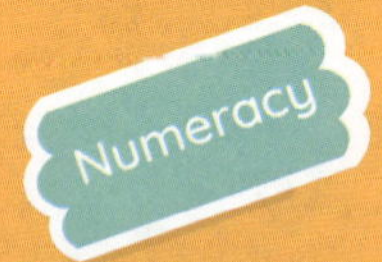

Circle the hidden numbers

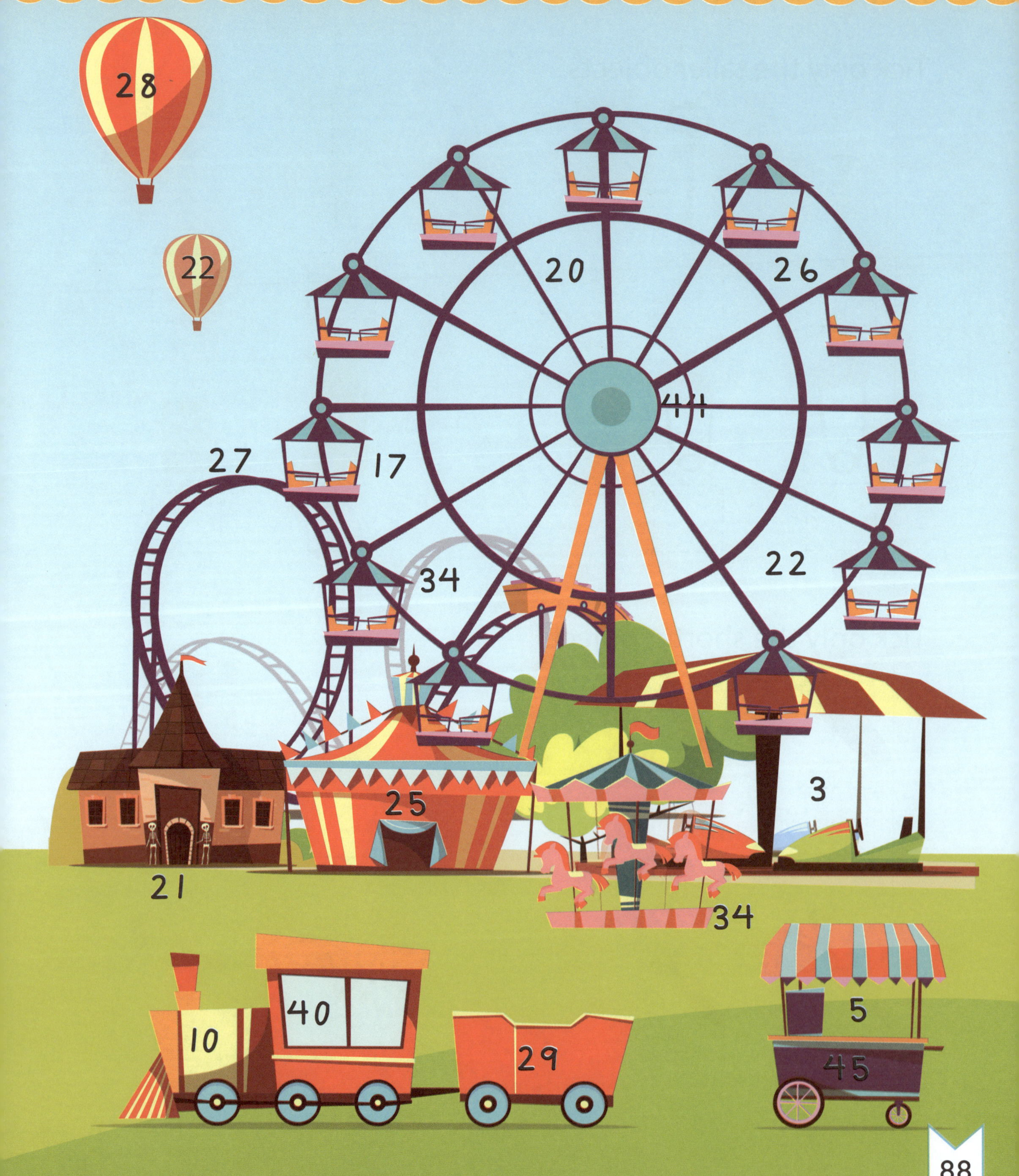

28
22
20
26
44
27
17
34
22
3
25
21
34
40
10
29
5
45

Find which numbers are greater, less or equal and put the correct sign >, <, =

15	....	18	31	....	25
20	....	4	46	....	38
12	....	12	37	....	39
17	....	20	41	....	41
24	....	32	39	....	43
27	....	16	50	....	37
19	....	12	26	....	22
11	....	16	50	....	50
18	....	18	24	....	37
24	....	20	43	....	45

Write the missing numbers

1		3		5			8
9		11		13			16
17		19		21			24
25		27		29			32
33		35		37			40
41		43		45			48

49 50

Find the Differences

3 - 1 = 2

4 - 2 =

3 - 3 =

5 - 2 =

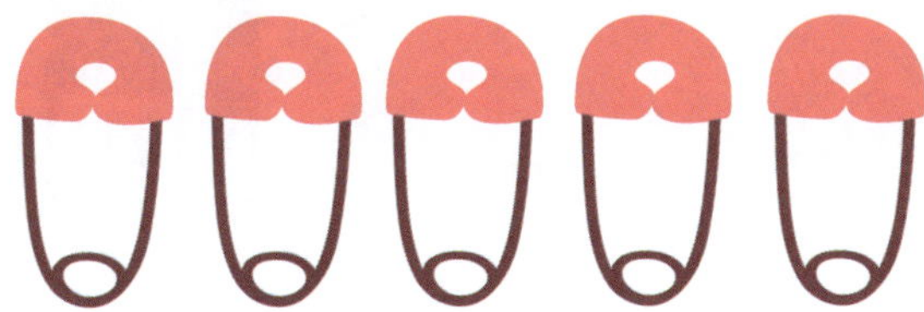

5 - 4 =

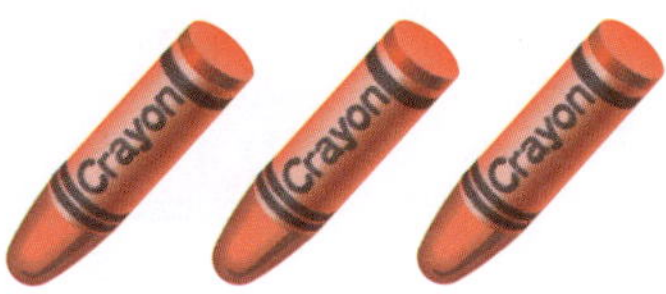

3 - 1 =

7 - 4 =

Match the missing part of the houses

Find the sum of the objects

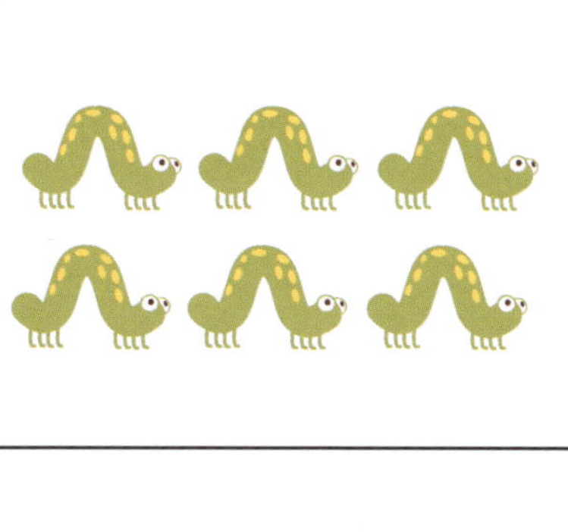		$6 + 3 =$ 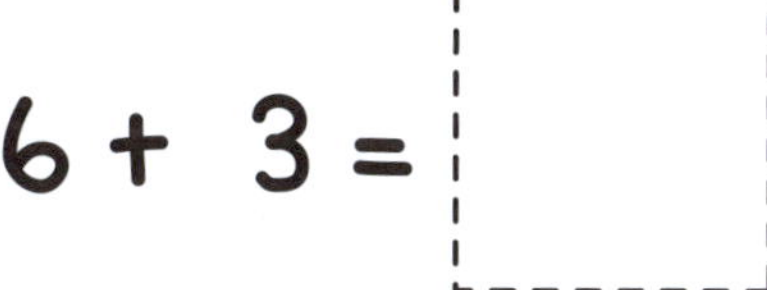	
		$3 + 2 =$	
		$2 + 1 =$	
		$4 + 3 =$	
		$5 + 2 =$	

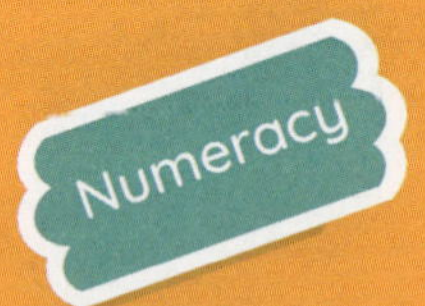

Count the number of pictures in each row and circle the correct number

	2	1
	7	5
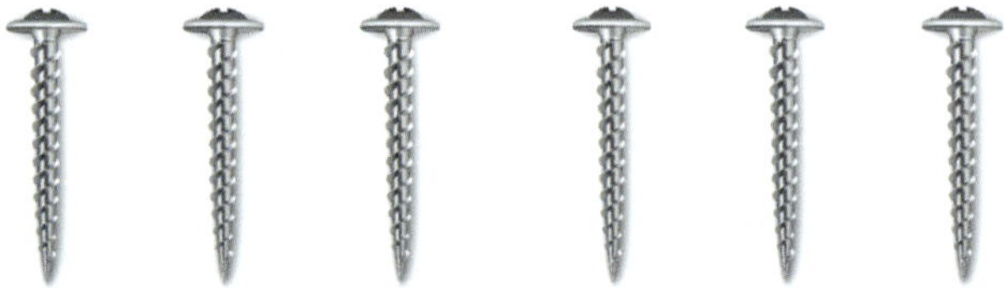	6	8
	7	5
	8	6
	7	9

Numeracy

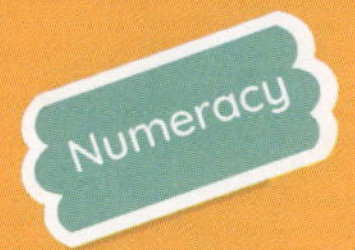

Put the correct sign greater than, less than or equal to (>, <, =)

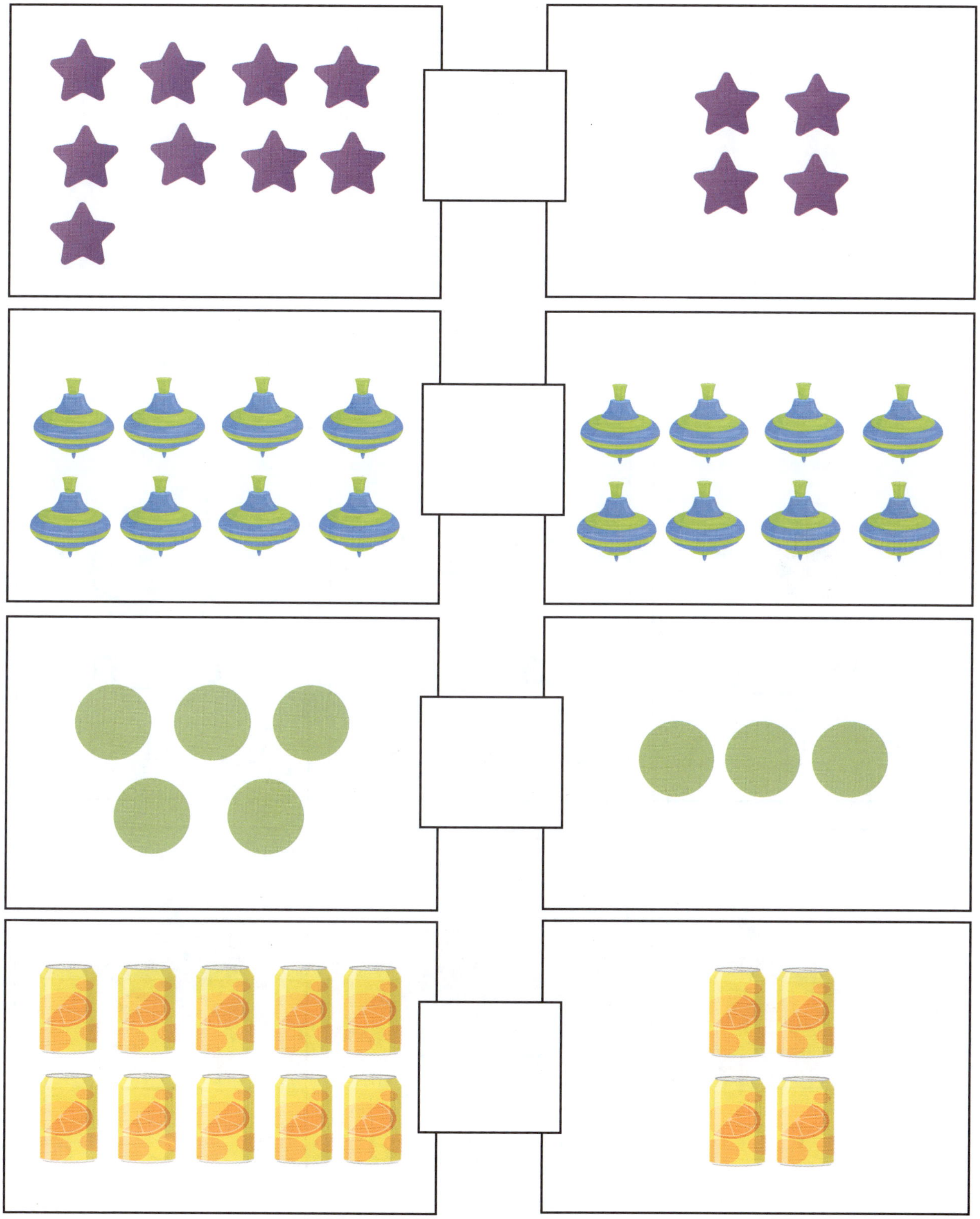

Look at the pictures and complete the word

f___n

e u a

p___n

i u a

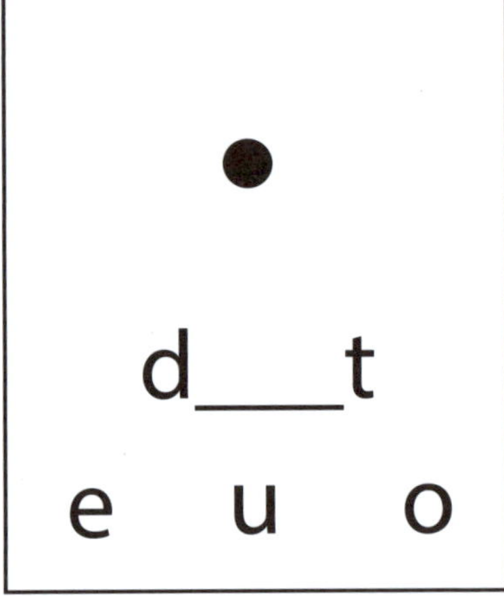

d___t

e u o

b___g

e u a

m___p

e u a

t___n

e u a

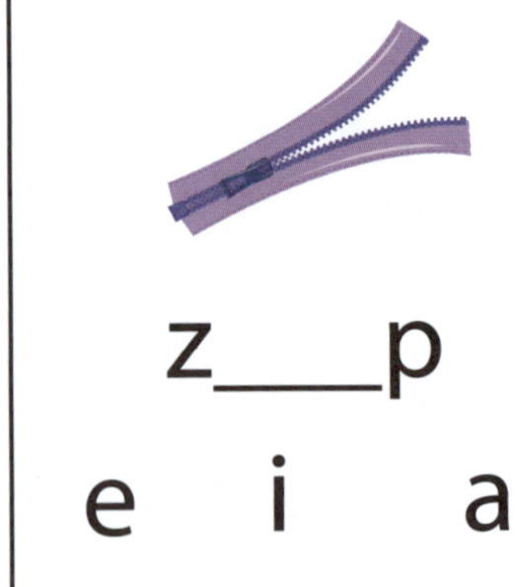

z___p

e i a

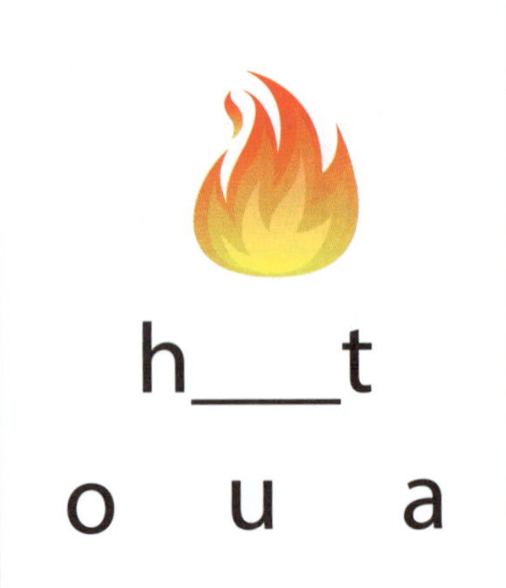

h___t

o u a

t___b

e u a

Trace the numbers 0-5 and tick the correct spelling

5

five ☐

two ☐

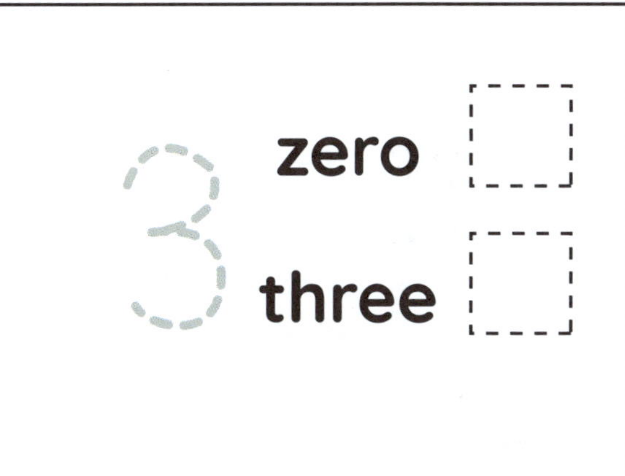

1

two ☐

one ☐

0

zero ☐

one ☐

2

two ☐

five ☐

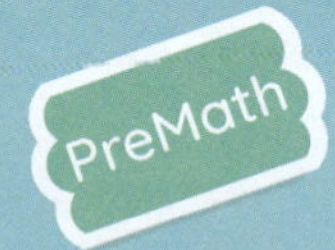

Match the opposites

short

close

hot

top

open

cold

bottom

tall

Read and circle the odd one out

met	set	let	win
tap	dot	map	lap
lip	hip	sip	won
mat	dog	fog	jog
bug	pig	rug	mug
bad	mad	had	wet
ten	mat	hen	pen

Look at the picture and colour the correct word

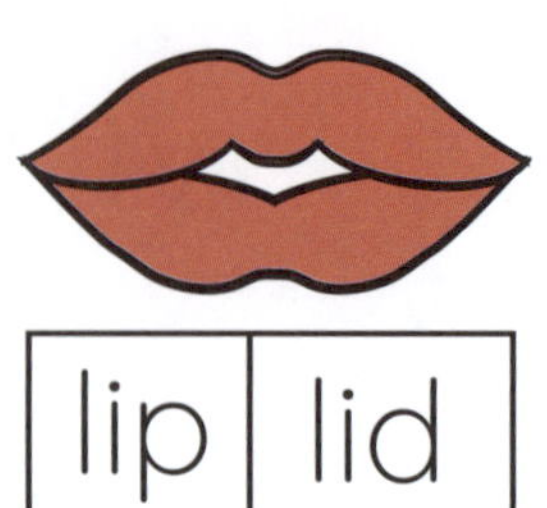

lip | lid

fin | fig

lid | kit

pin | pig

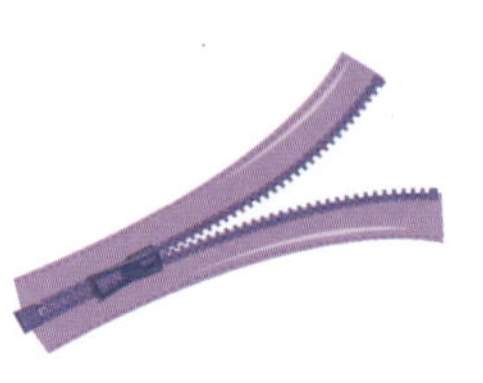

mix | mid

pit | pin

kid | kit

Rearrange and match the letters to the pictures

acp **cap** ----------

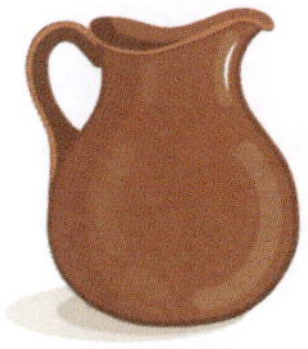

nip ----------

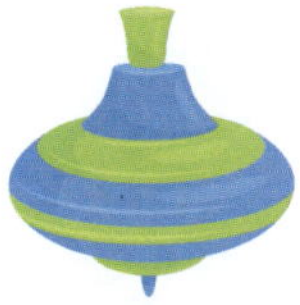

tac ----------

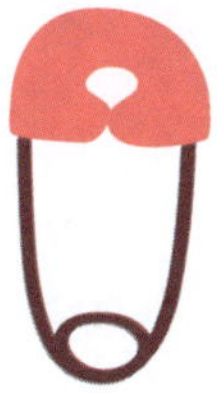

nug ----------

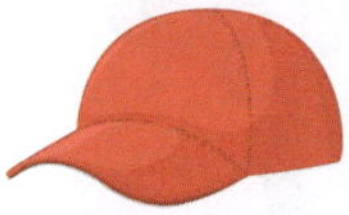

ocp ----------

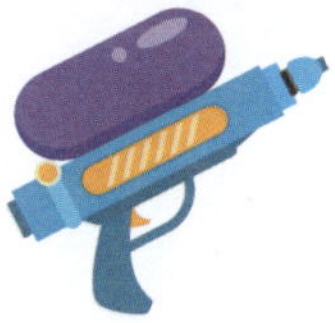

otp ----------

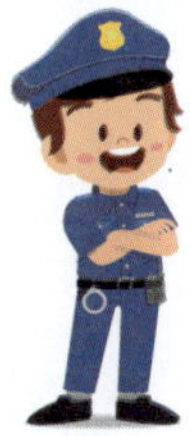

guj ----------

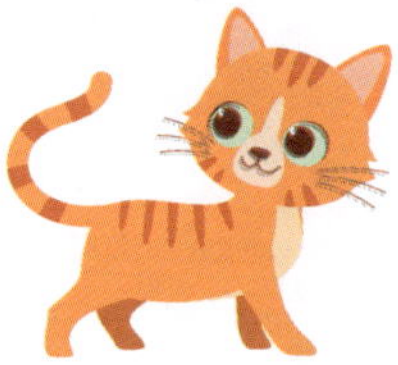

Write a/an looking at the picture

an orange

-------igloo

-------apple

------- banana

------- bear

-------flower

-------rabbit

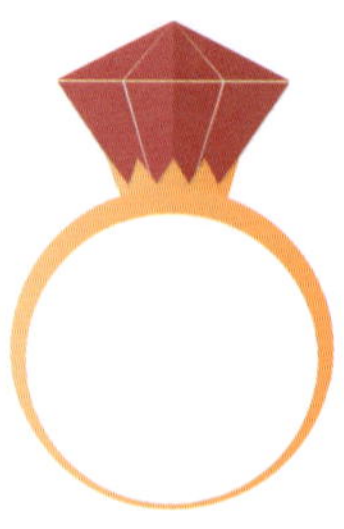

------- ring

------- elephant

------- eraser

Spot the five differences

Cognitive development

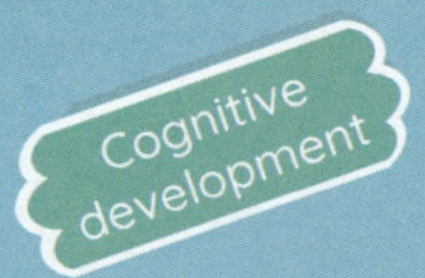

Circle the below-given parts of animals in the zoo

gorilla

giraffe

Panda

snake

bear

fox

lion

duck

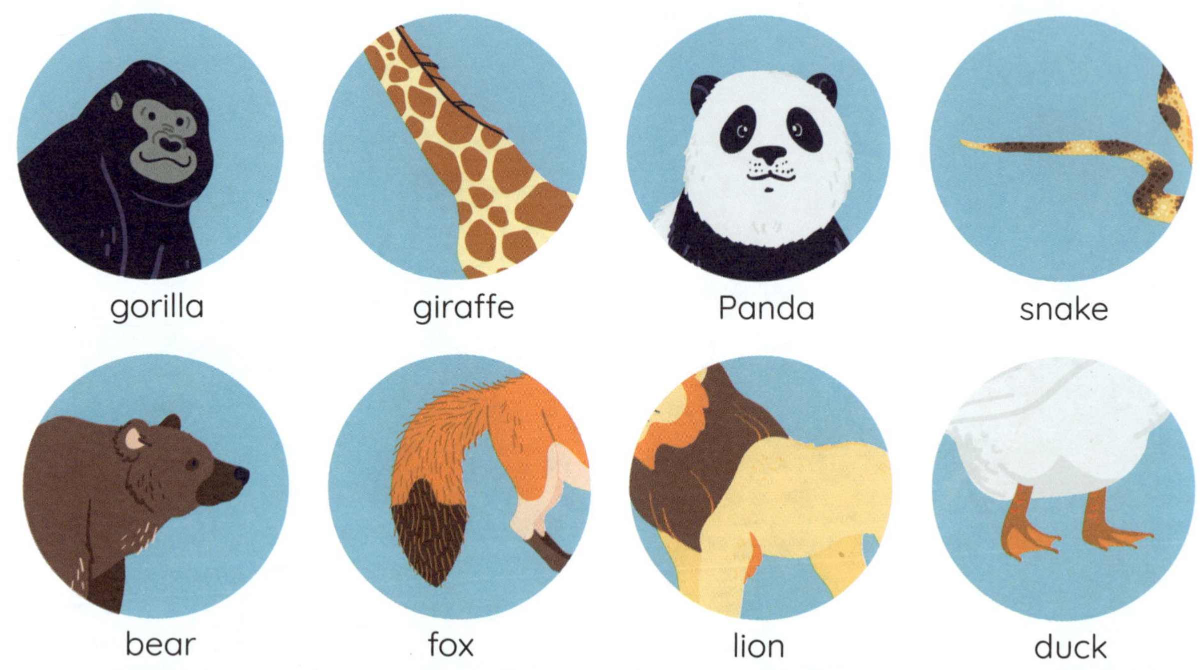

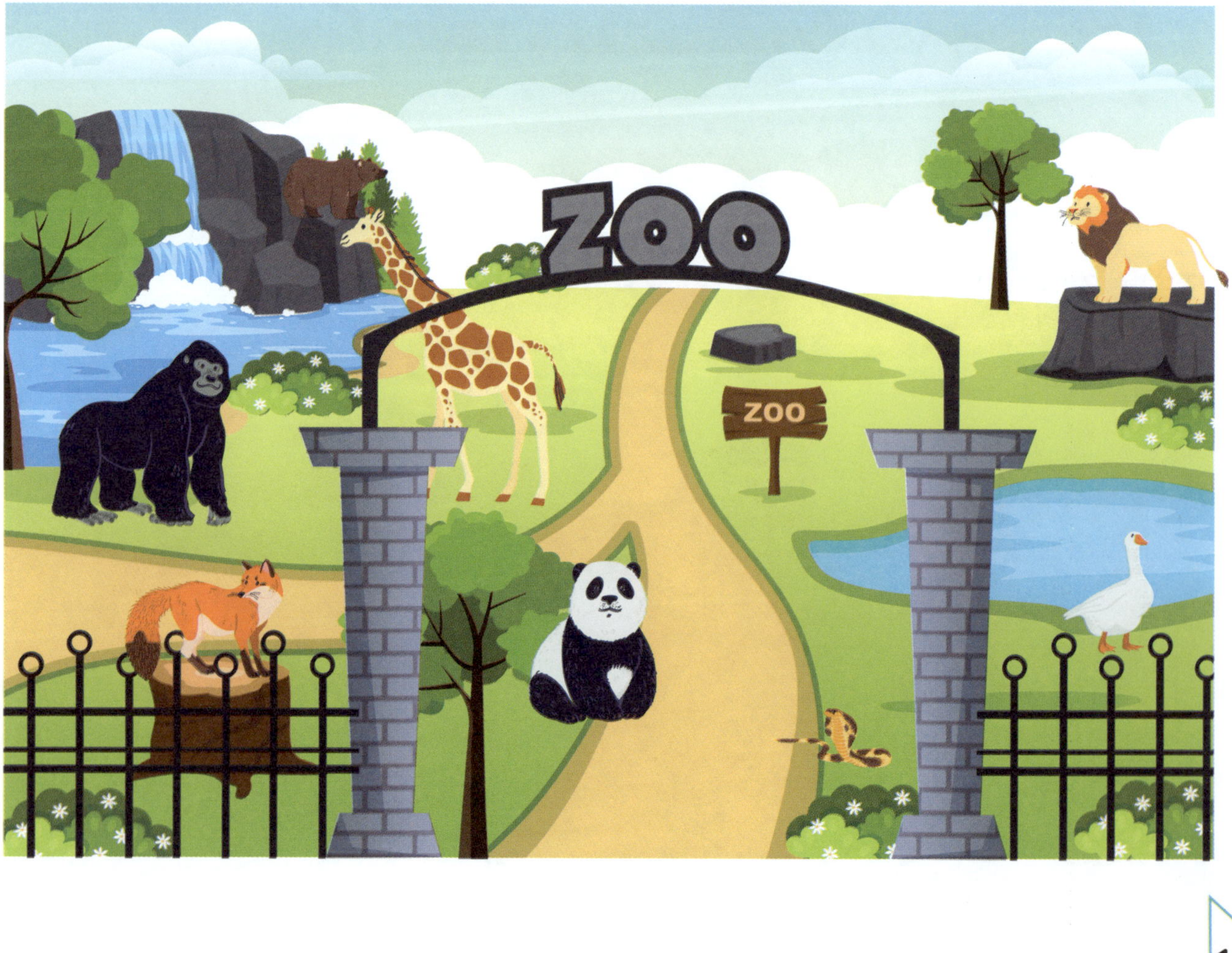

Fill in the missing letters

s______n

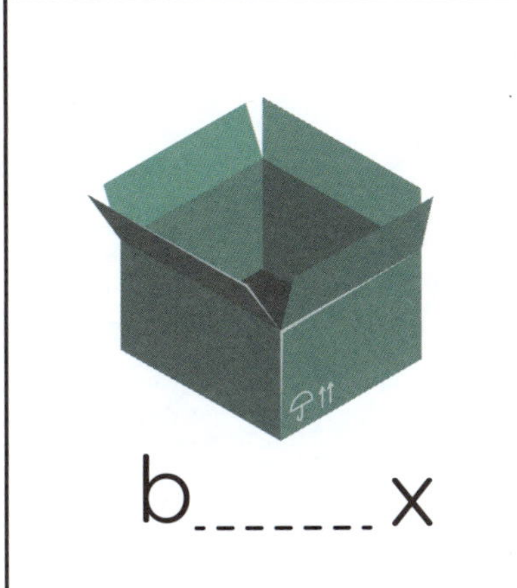

b______x

b_____r d

d_____g

f______s h

s t_____r

k_____y

b_____d

b_____l l

Colour the pictures following the instructions

The umbrella is blue and white

The flower is red and yellow

I see big, yellow sun

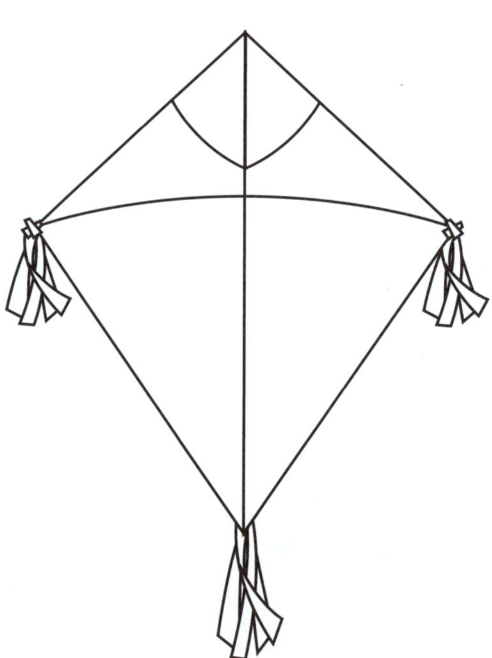

I have a green and purple kite

Complete the puzzle by writing the missing letters in the words

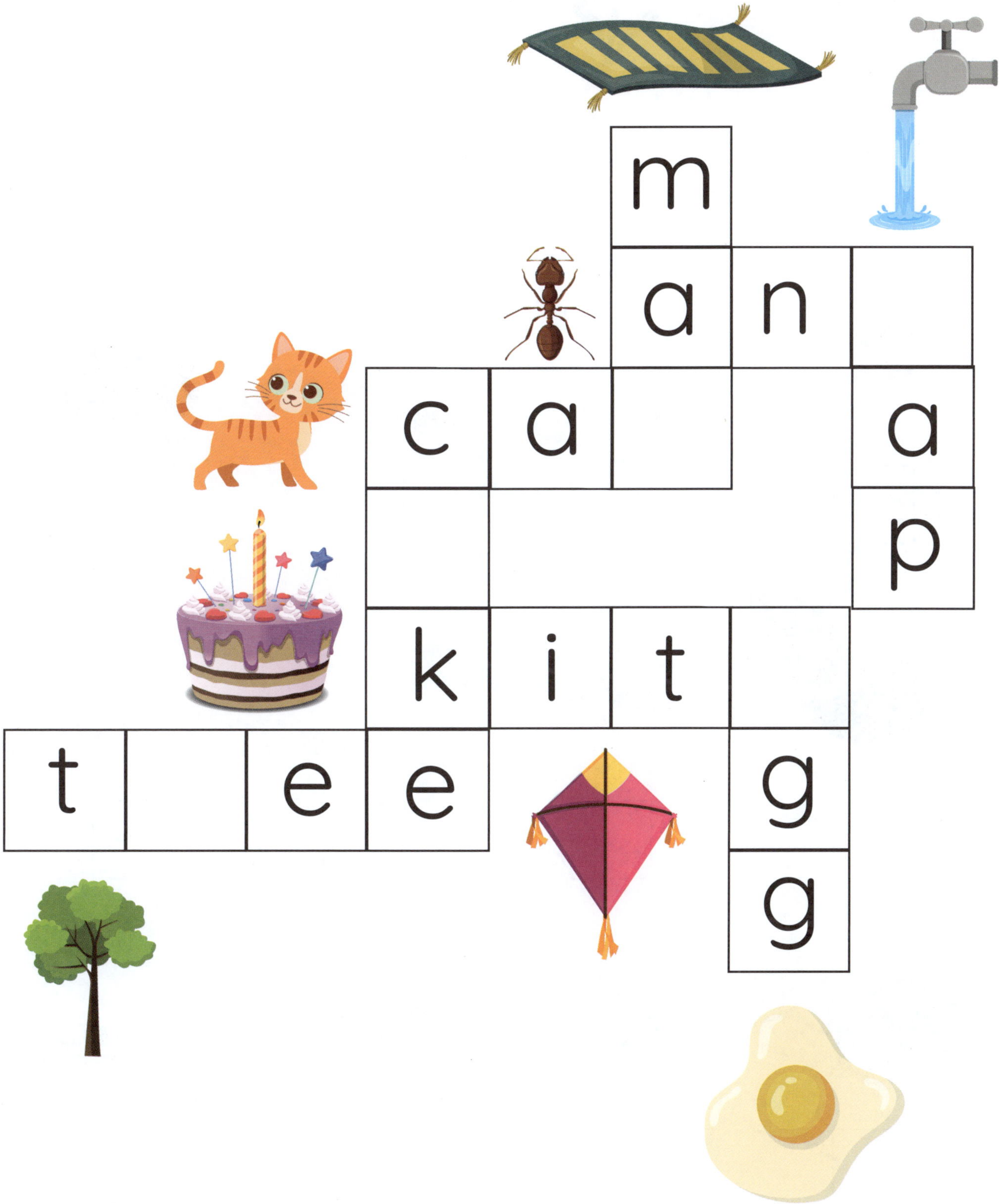

					m		
					a	n	
			c	a			a
							p
			k	i	t		
t		e	e			g	
						g	

EVS

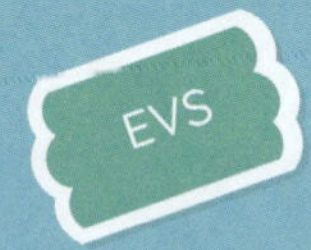

Tick the vegetables that grow underground

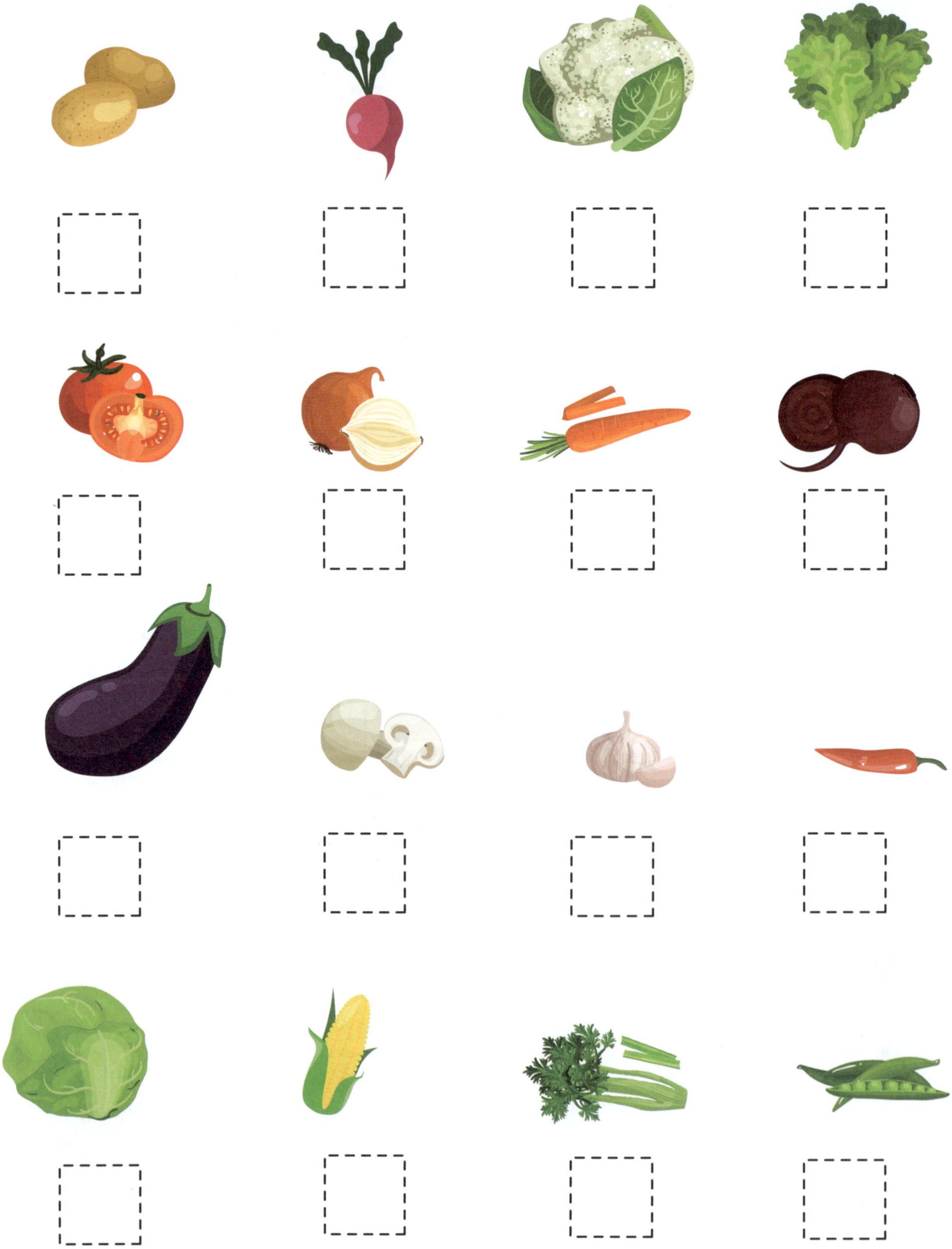

Read the word and circle the correct picture

cat 

den  

pin 

box   

run   

dot   

Select “a” ”an” or “the” for each sentence and colour the box

1. It is | a | an | the | elephant.

2. | a | an | the | pink dress is mine.

3. It is | a | an | the | cat.

4. It is | a | an | the | house.

5. Look at | a | an | the | stars.

6. It is | a | an | the | owl.

7. It is | a | an | the | umbrella.

8. | a | an | the | sky is blue.

Literacy

Write the middle letter to complete the word

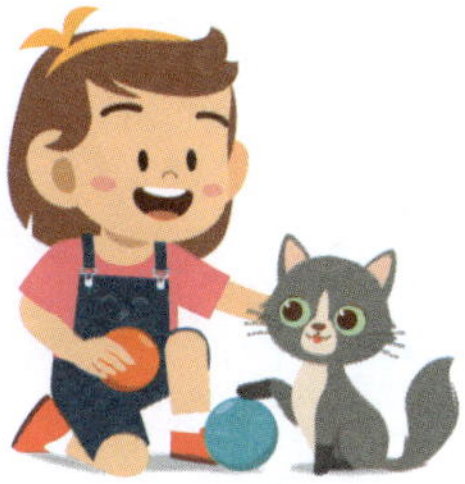

p ☐ t

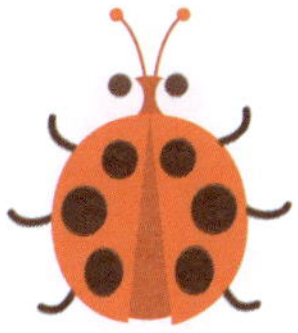

b ☐ g

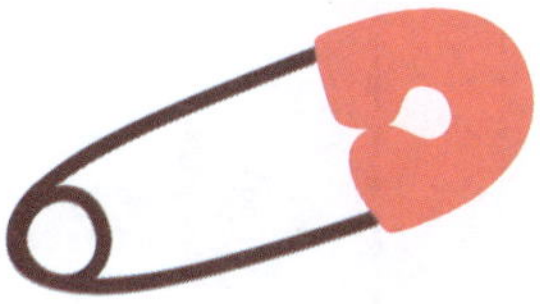

p ☐ n

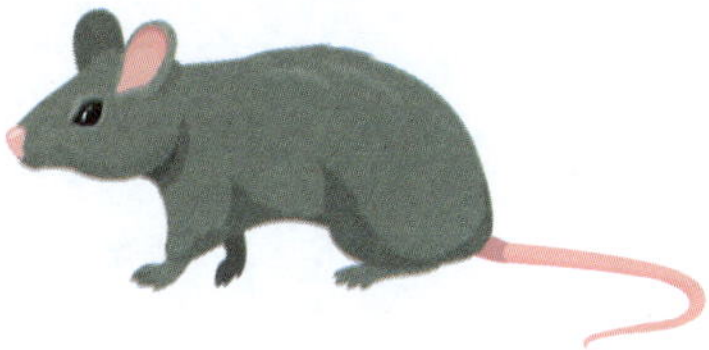

r ☐ t

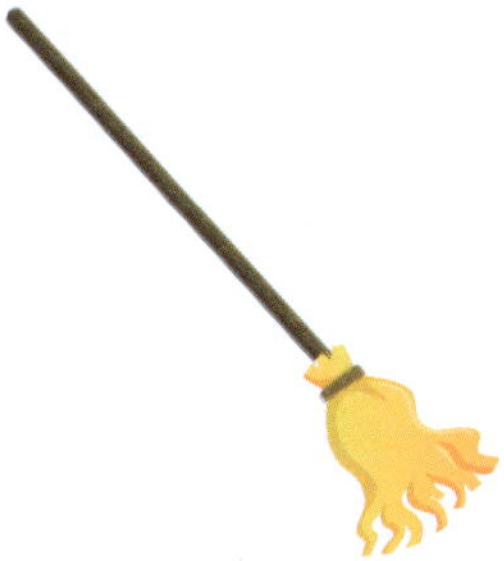

m ☐ p

a e i o u

Match the fish to their direction

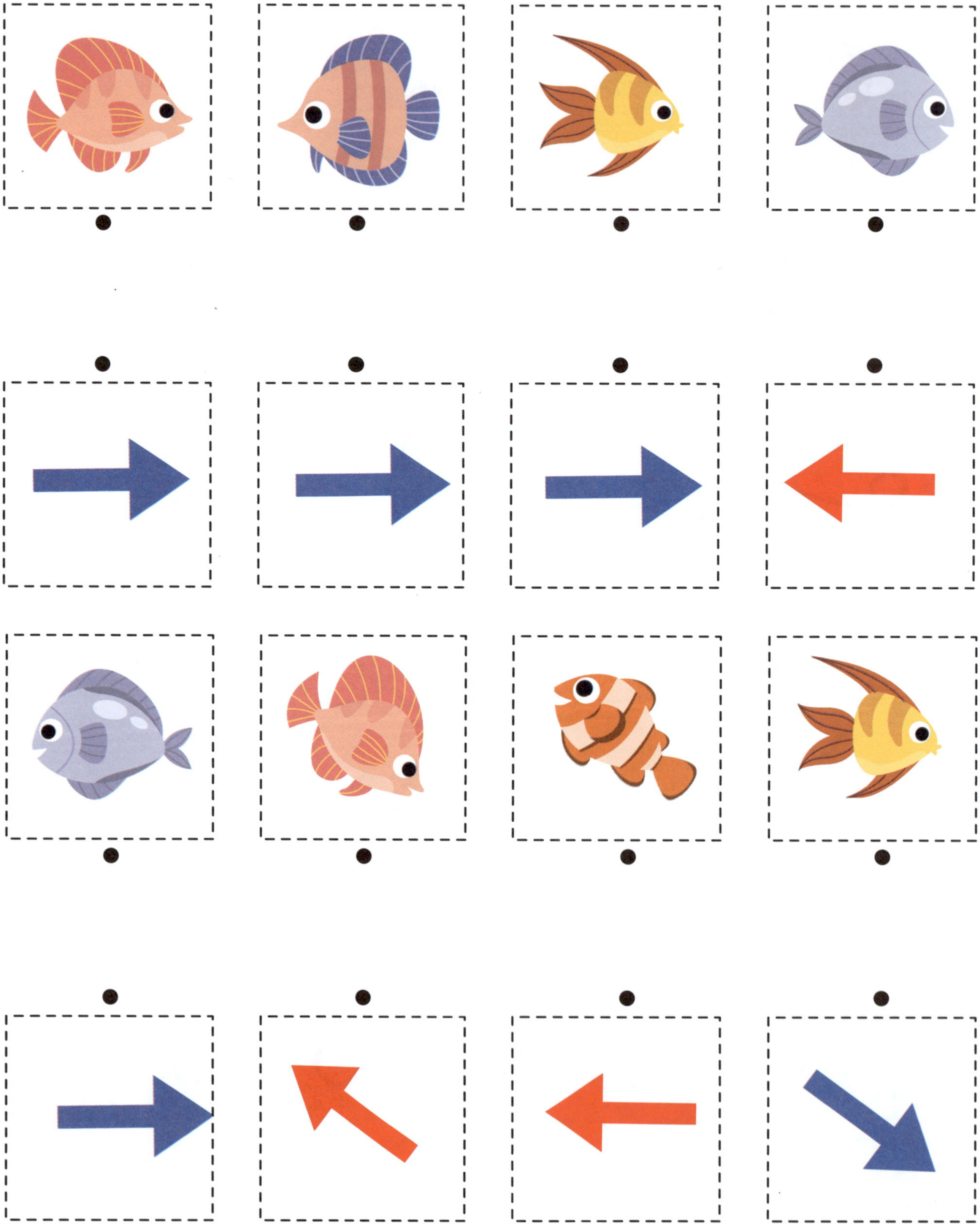

Complete the sentence using 'and'

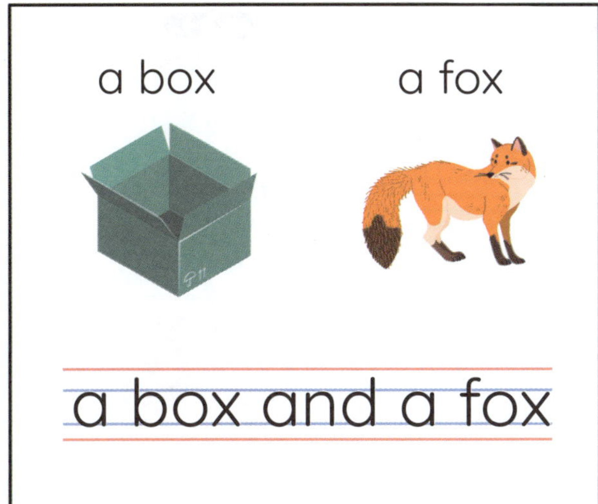

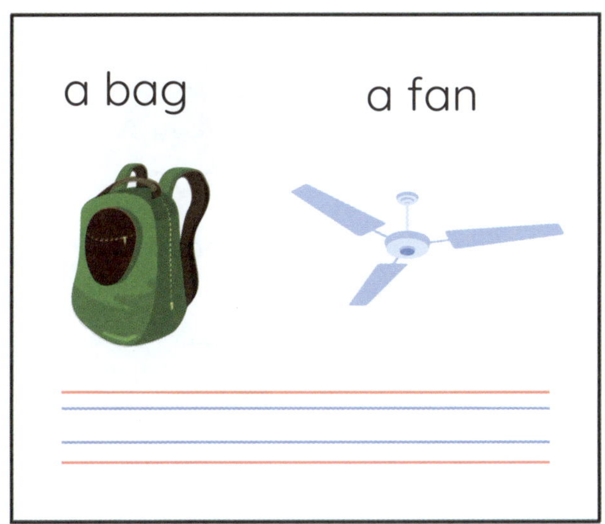

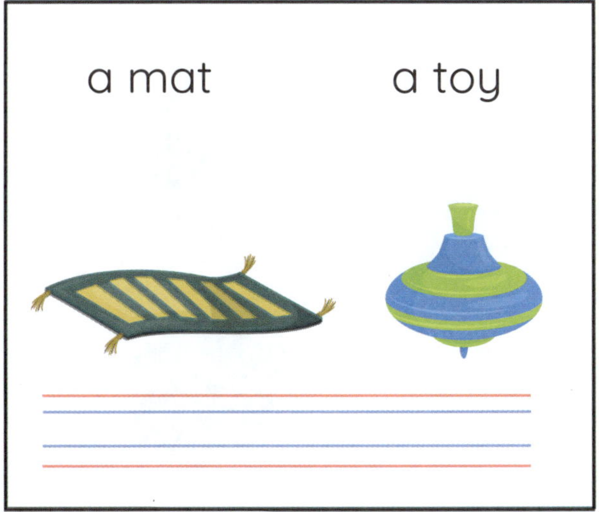

Match the rhyming words

bed

jar

bee

red

bug

tree

car

mug

fox

bin

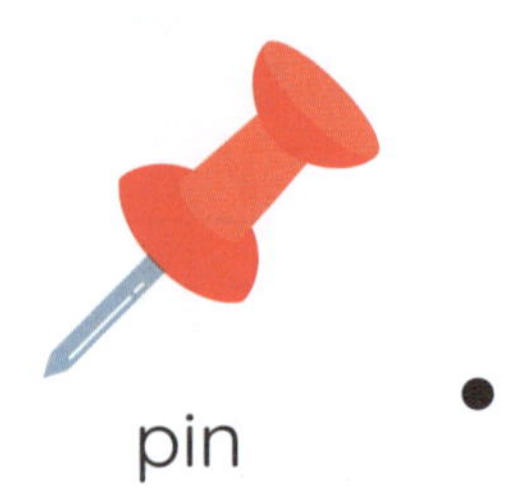

pin

box

Fill in the blanks with the correct articles

a	an

1.  ----- cat

2.  ----- elephant

3.  ----- cake

4. 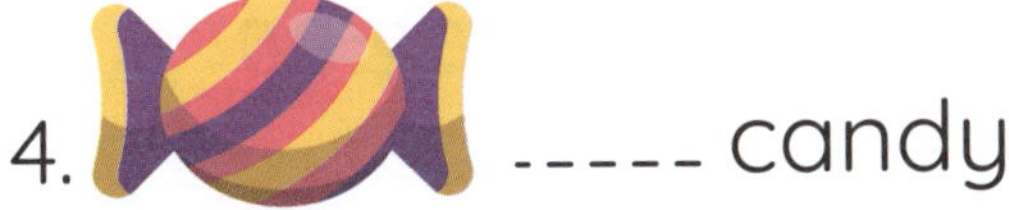 ----- candy

5.  ----- egg

6.  ----- tree

7.    ----- eye

8.  ----- ball

9.  ----- book

10.  ----- orange

11.  ----- eraser

12.  ----- dog

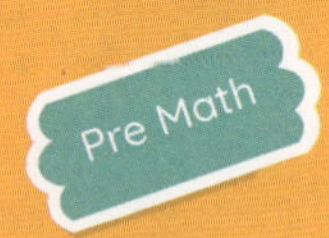

Draw hands on the clock's face to show the time

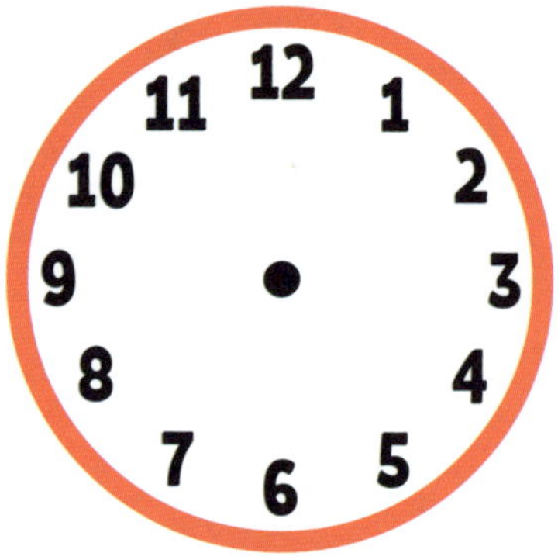

09:00	01:00	11:00
04:00	07:00	02:00
05:00	12:00	03:00

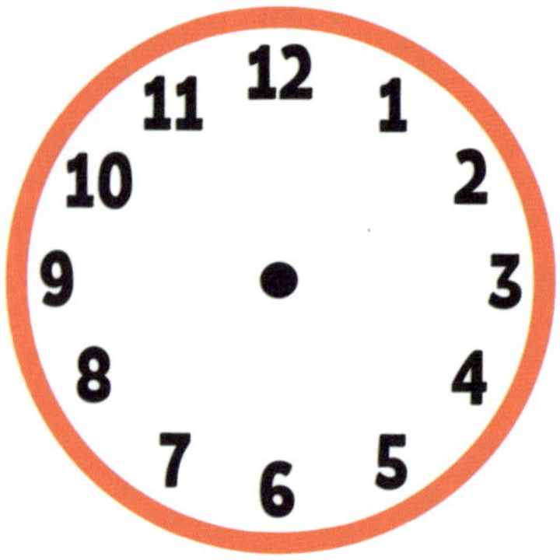

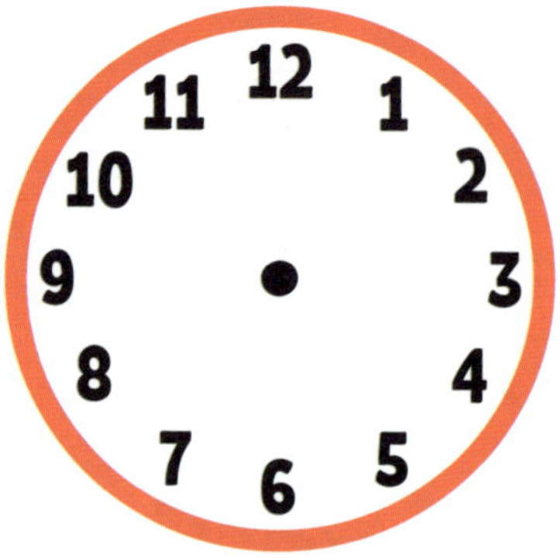

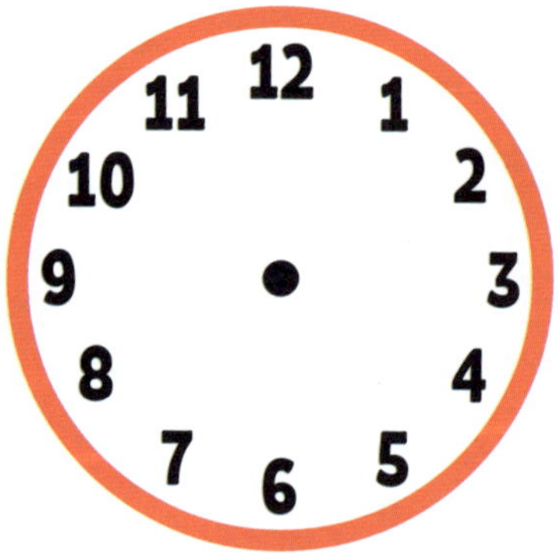

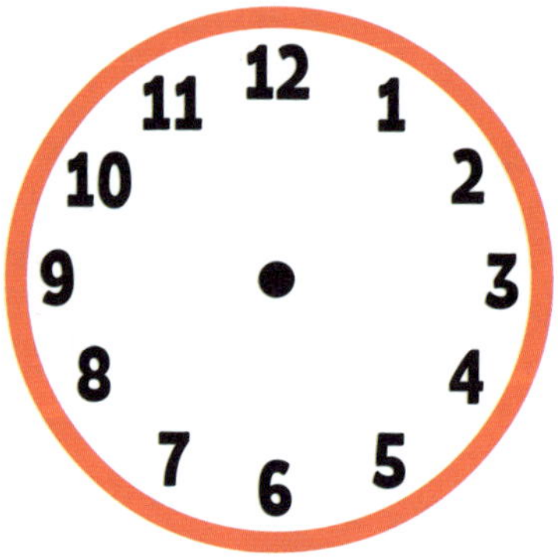

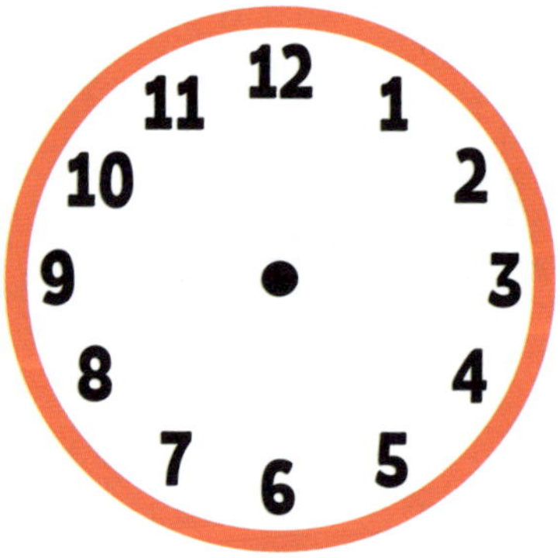

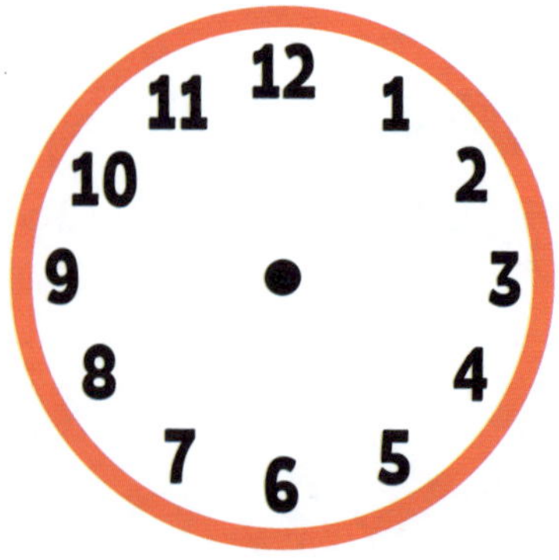

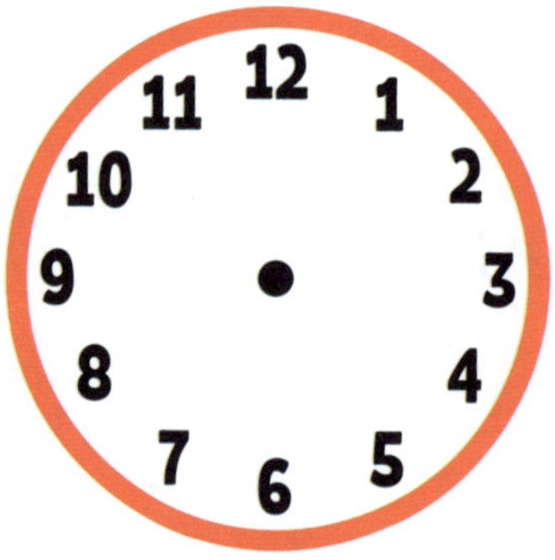

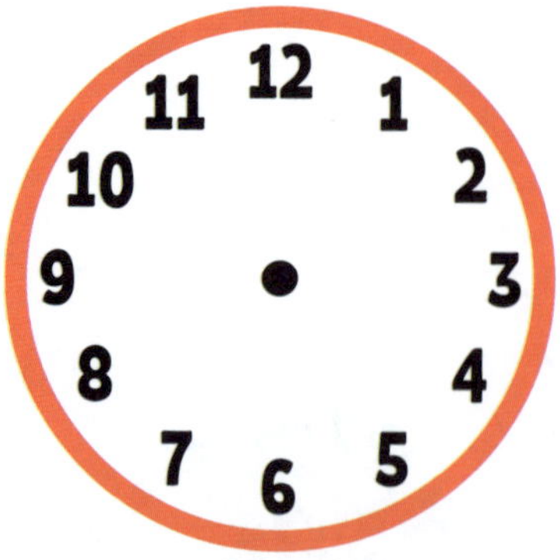

Add each group and write the answer in the given box

4 + 5 = ☐

3 + 4 = ☐

5 + 3 = ☐

3 + 1 = ☐

4 + 2 = ☐

two •	• 

five •	• 

three •	• 

one •	• 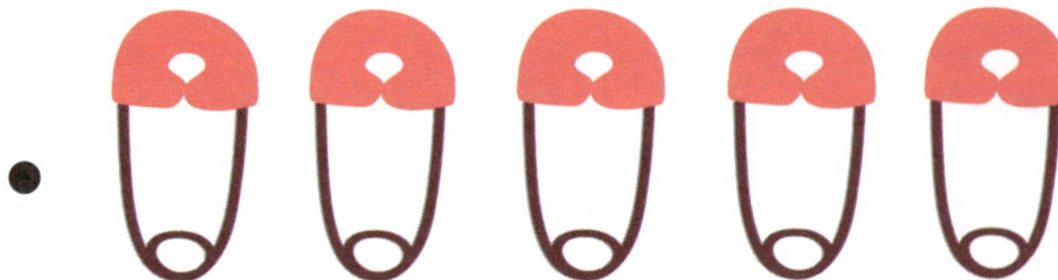

four •	• 

Numeracy

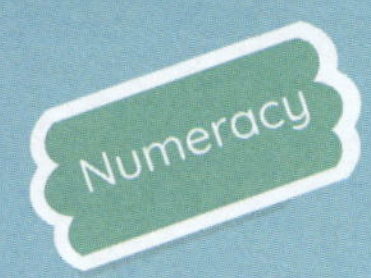

Count and put the correct sign

>	=	<

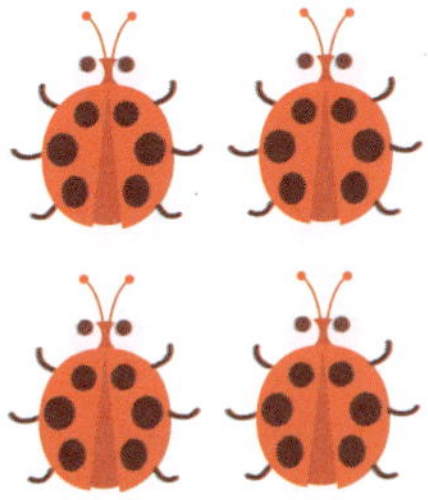

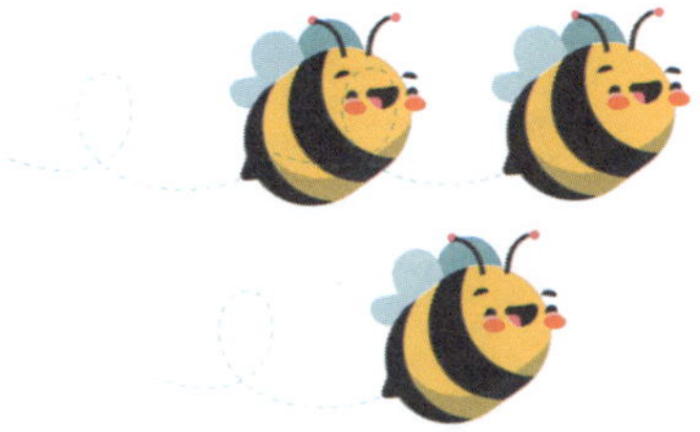

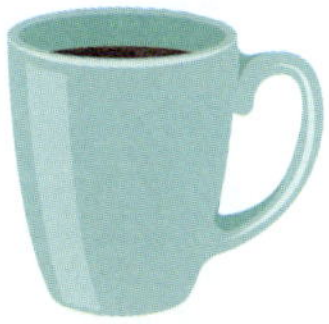

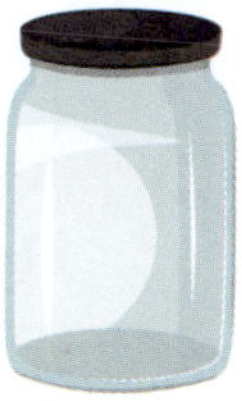

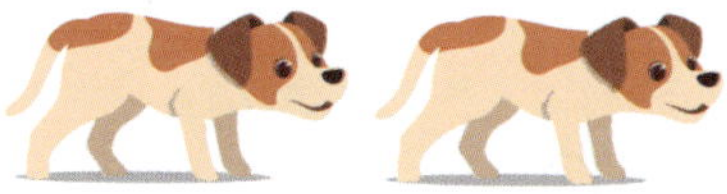

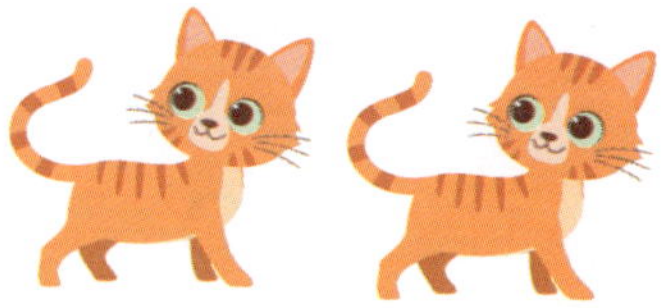

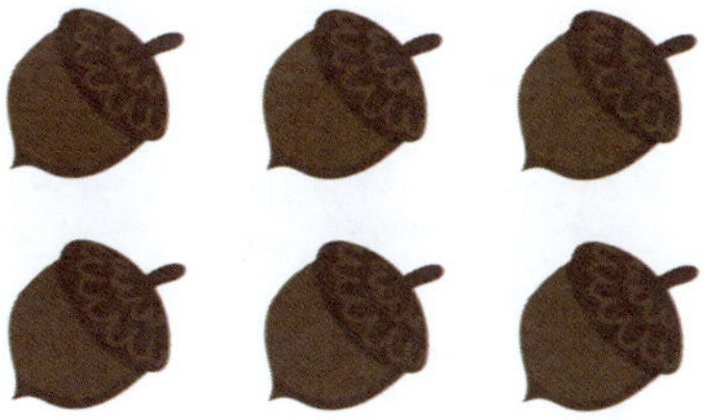

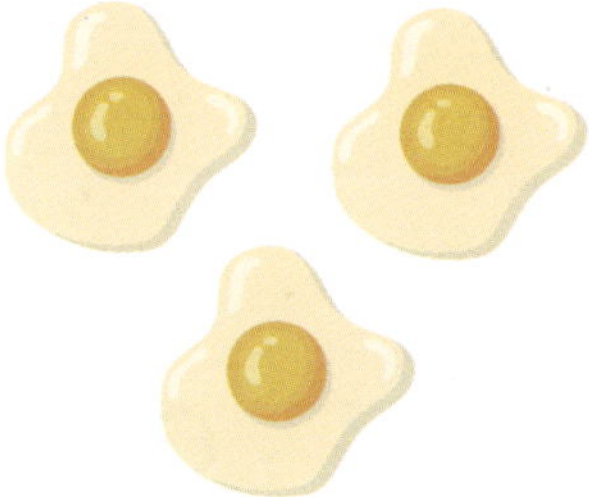

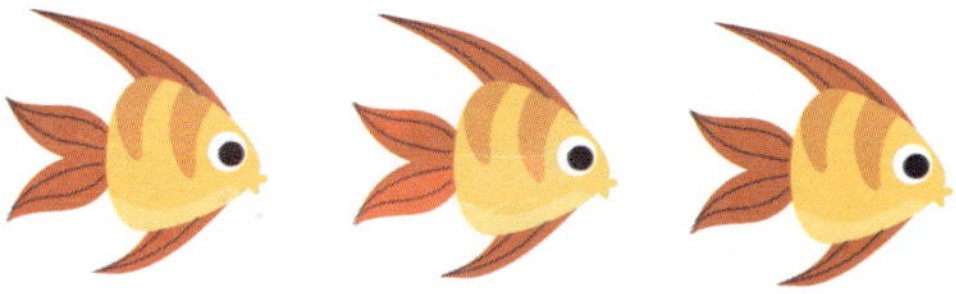

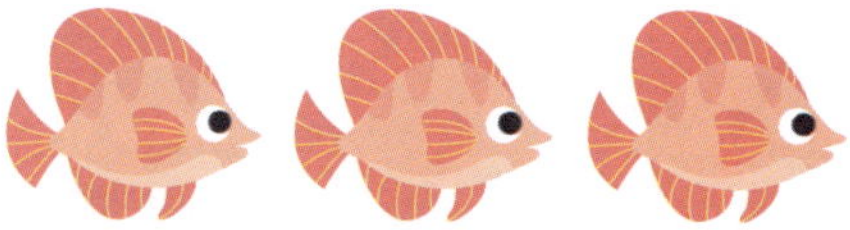

Numeracy

Write the correct number names

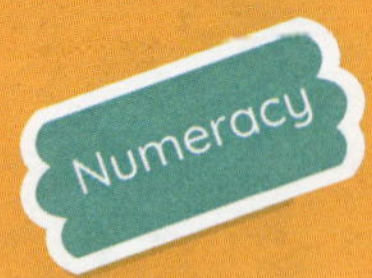

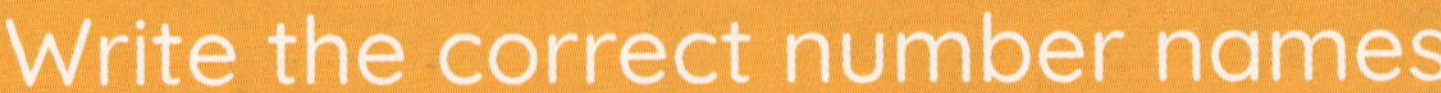

1 o n e

6 s x i

2 o w t

7 s e e v n

3 r h t e e

8 e t h i g

4 o u r f

9 n i n e

5 e v f i

10 e n t

Find and circle the three letter words hidden in the puzzle

cat	mop	fat	sad	van
rat	hat	fan	jam	tan

h	k	p	e	l	m	s	t	z	t
q	k	c	u	g	d	o	c	b	r
t	h	a	q	f	a	n	p	q	r
m	n	t	s	e	t	v	q	a	q
g	m	h	a	v	q	a	t	n	l
s	n	a	d	q	b	n	s	h	e
a	r	t	a	n	d	a	a	c	g
g	y	g	e	d	g	b	j	q	g
u	k	f	a	t	h	j	a	a	n
s	q	i	e	a	r	h	m	e	s

Number the pictures in a correct sequence

Unscramble the letters to form a word that matches the picture

odg → ____________

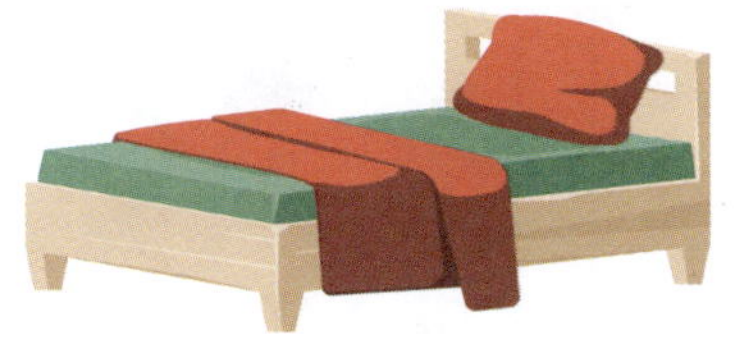

2. deb → ____________

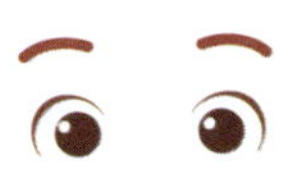

3. yee → ____________

4. pcu → ____________

5. tam → ____________

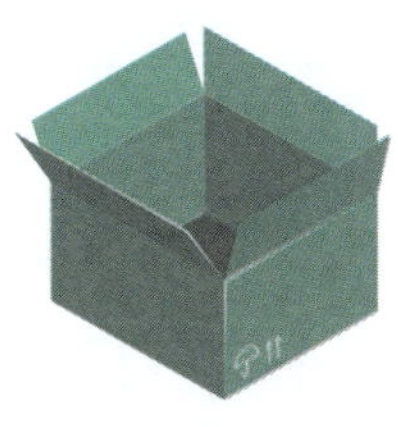

6. xbo → ____________

Answer sheet

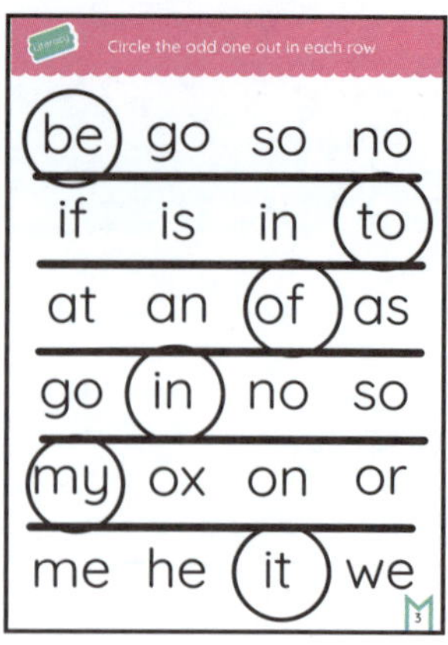

Pg no. 3

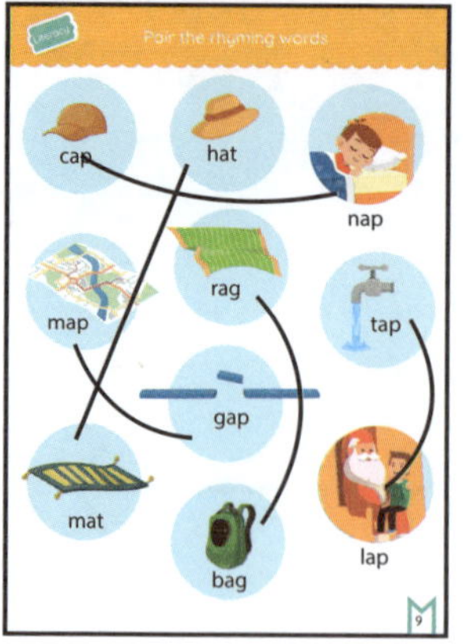

Pg no. 9

Pg no. 10

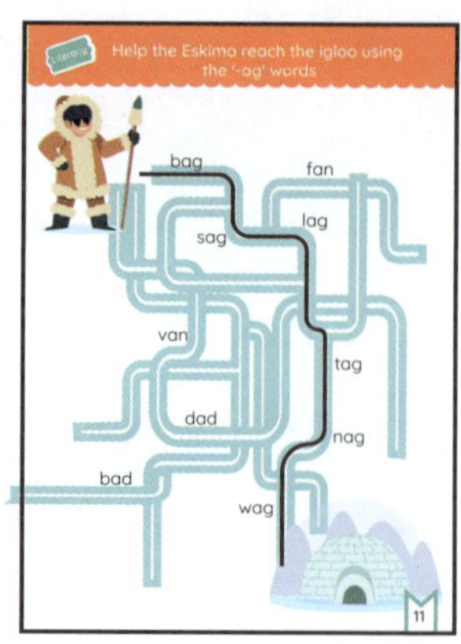

Pg no. 11

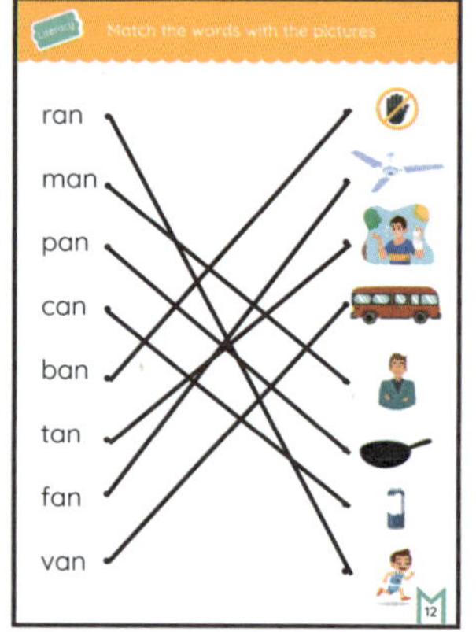

Pg no. 12

Pg no. 13

Pg no. 14

Pg no. 15

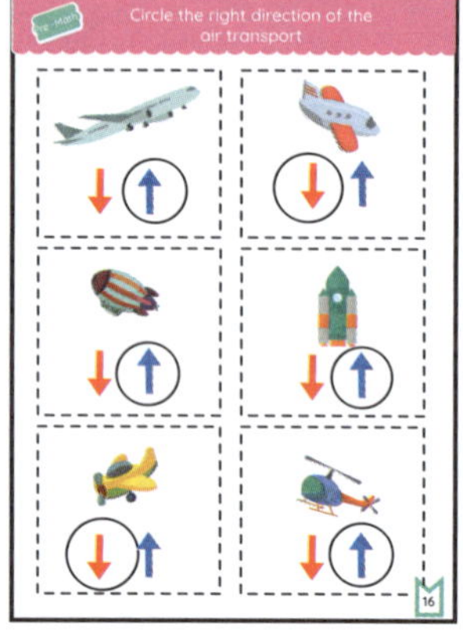

Pg no. 16

Pg no. 17

Pg no. 18

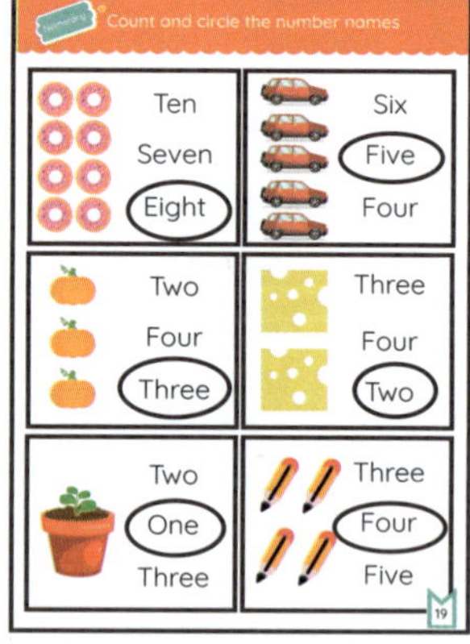

Pg no. 19

Pg no. 21

Pg no. 24

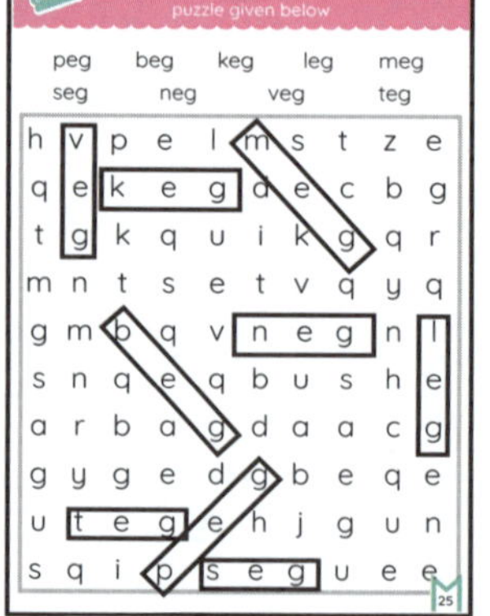

Pg no. 25

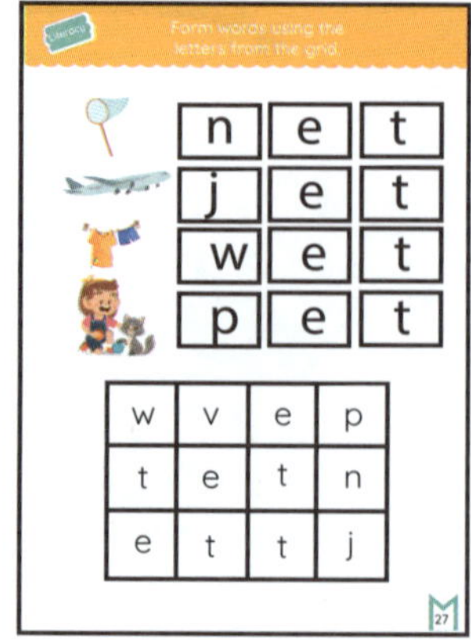

Pg no. 27

Pg no. 28

Pg no. 29

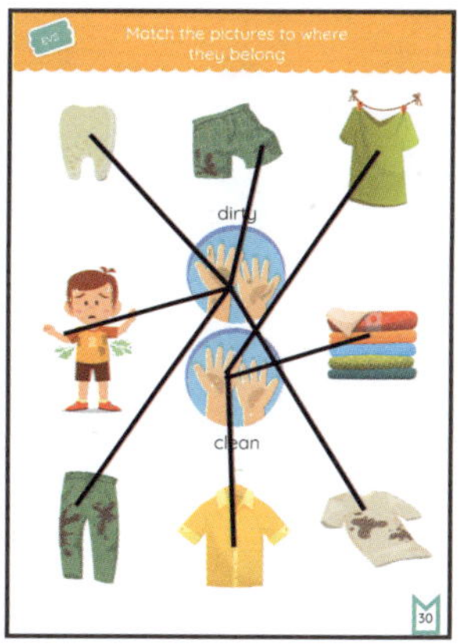

Pg no. 30

Pg no. 31

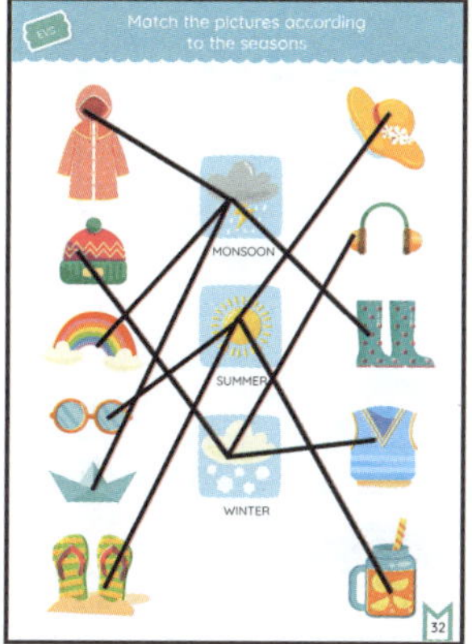

Pg no. 32

Pg no. 33

Pg no. 34

Pg no. 35

Pg no. 36

Pg no. 37

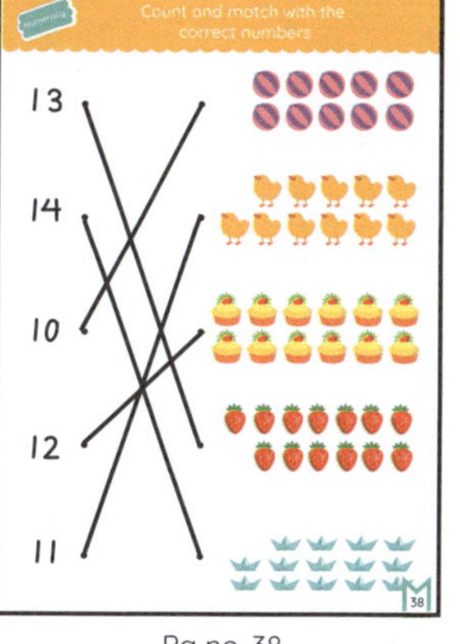

Pg no. 38

Pg no. 39

Pg no. 40

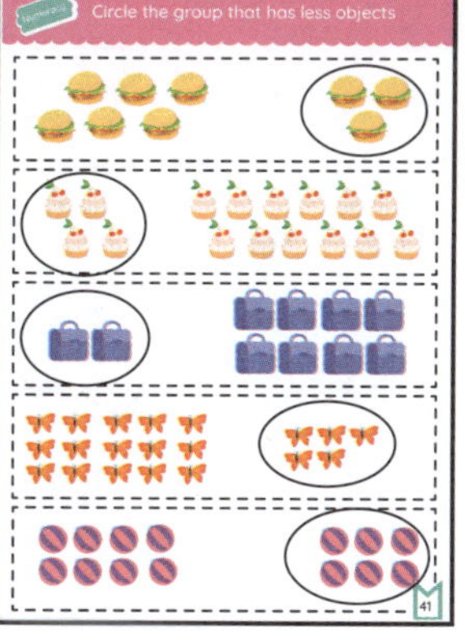

Pg no. 41

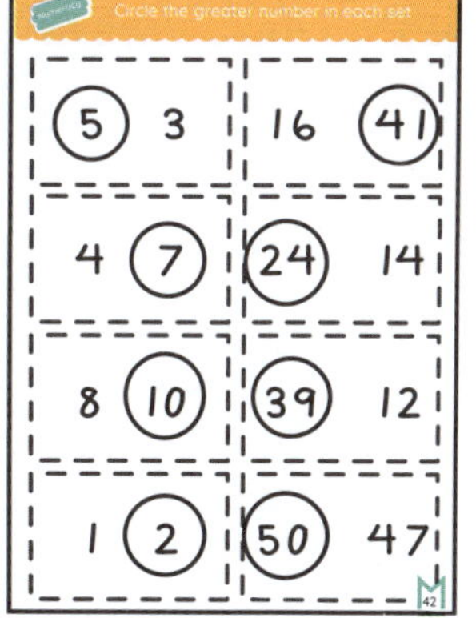

Pg no. 42

Pg no. 43

Pg no. 44

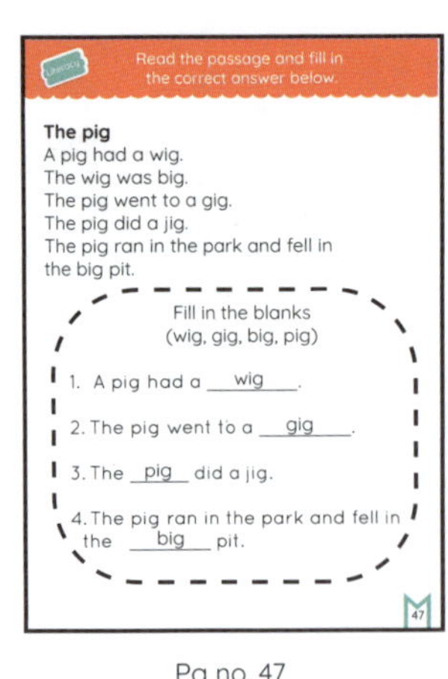
Pg no. 47

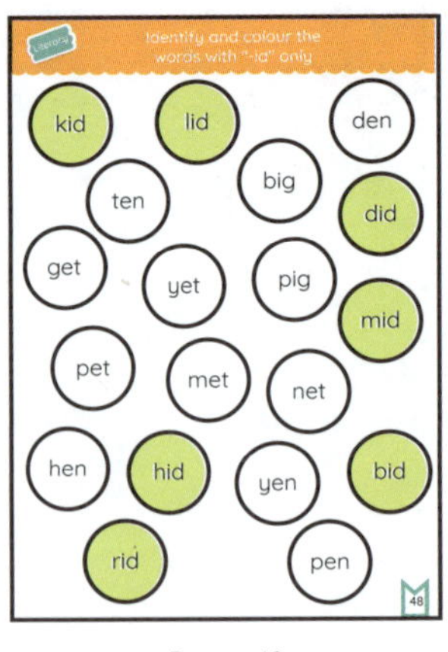
Pg no. 48

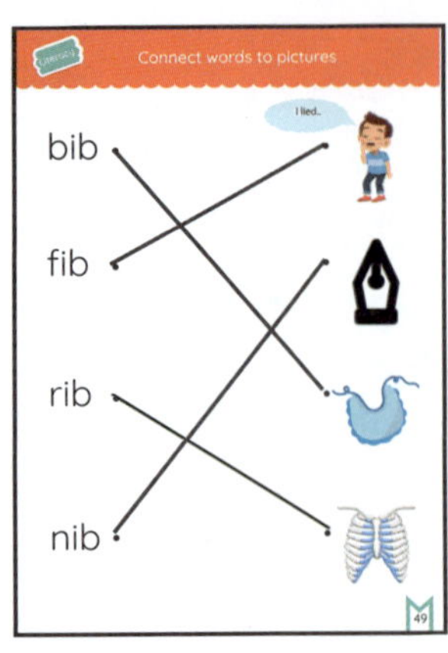
Pg no. 49

Pg no. 50

Pg no. 51

Pg no. 52

Pg no. 53

Pg no. 54

Pg no. 55

Pg no. 56

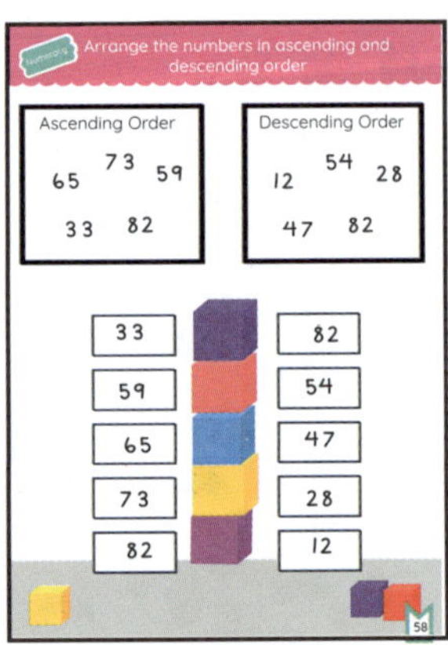
Pg no. 58

Pg no. 60

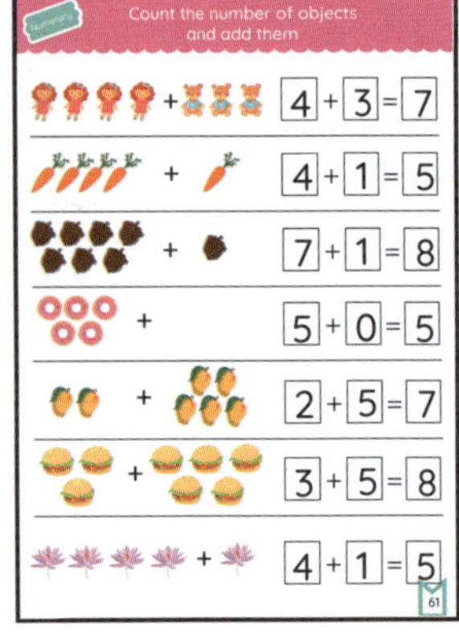
Pg no. 61

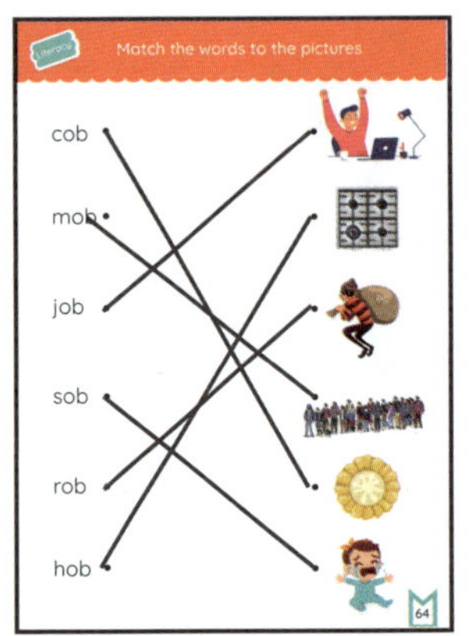
Pg no. 64

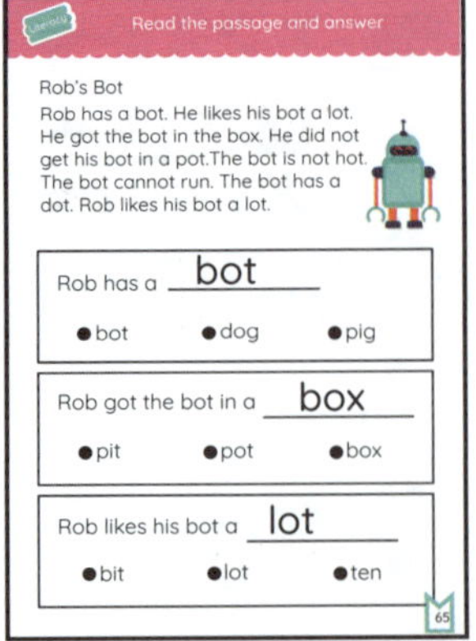
Pg no. 65

Trace the first letters and connect the words to the pictures

sod

cod

nod

pod

rod

66

Pg no. 66

Write the correct words

top hop cop mop pop stop

I use a mop to clean

I like to hop in the air!

I can ask the cop for help.

The popcorn goes pop

STOP stop at the end of the road.

The man climbs to the top

67

Pg no. 67

Look at the picture and write the beginning letter to complete the word

dog

jog

log

hog

68

Pg no. 68

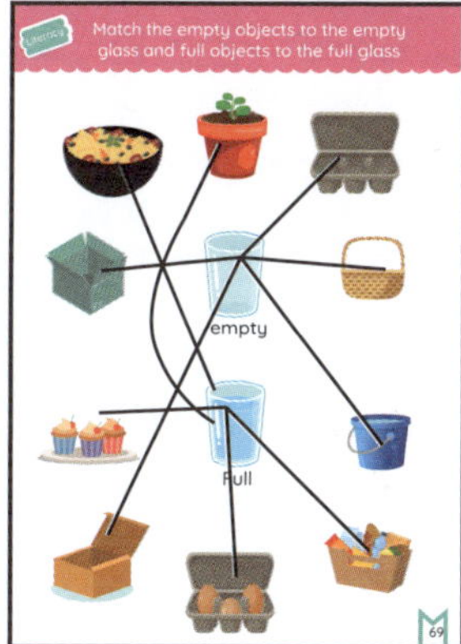
Match the empty objects to the empty glass and full objects to the full glass

empty

full

69

Pg no. 69

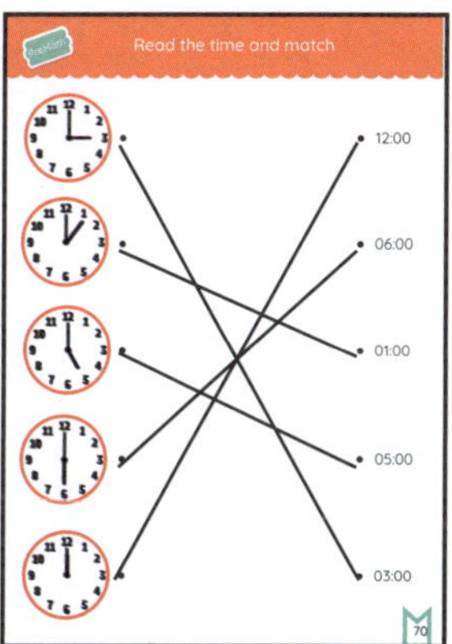
Read the time and match

12:00

06:00

01:00

05:00

03:00

70

Pg no. 70

Match these animals to their appropriate habitats

71

Pg no. 71

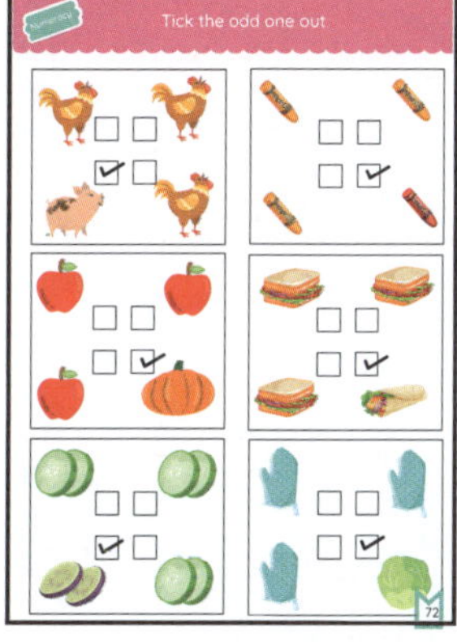
Tick the odd one out

72

Pg no. 72

Tick the healthy food item and cross the unhealthy food item

73

Pg no. 73

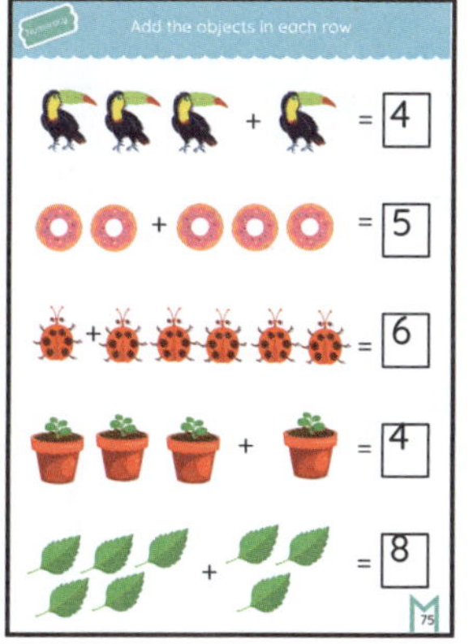
Add the objects in each row

= 4

= 5

= 6

= 4

= 8

75

Pg no. 75

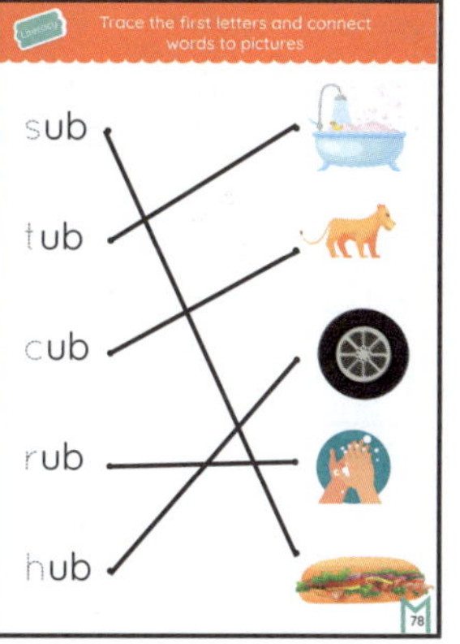
Trace the first letters and connect words to pictures

sub

tub

cub

rub

hub

78

Pg no. 78

Unscramble the words and write

u n b — bun

n s u — sun

u r n — run

g n u — gun

u n f — fun

u n n — nun

80

Pg no. 80

Write the begining letter and complete the word

hut

nut

cut

81

Pg no. 81

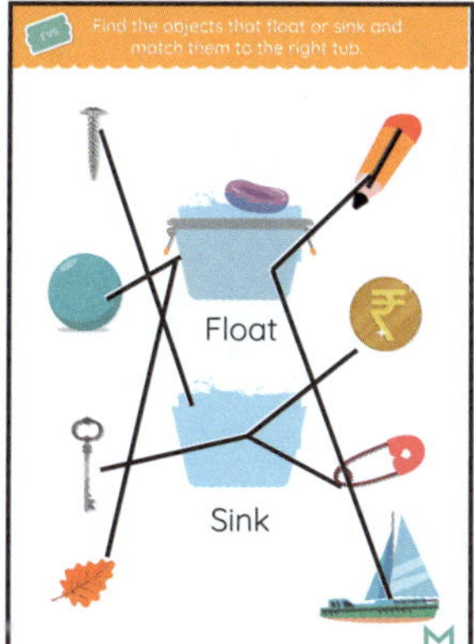
Find the objects that float or sink and match them to the right tub.

Float

Sink

82

Pg no. 82

Circle the activities that need water

83

Pg no. 83

Where do they belong?

Good Manners

Bad Manners

84

Pg no. 84

Trace a circle around the habitat of each animal.

85

Pg no. 85

Pg no. 87

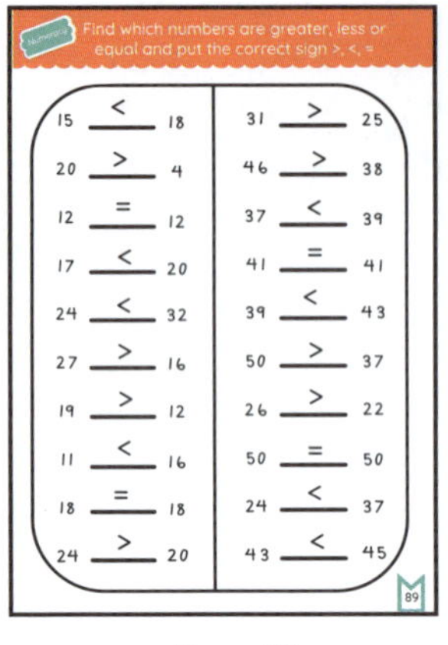

Pg no. 89

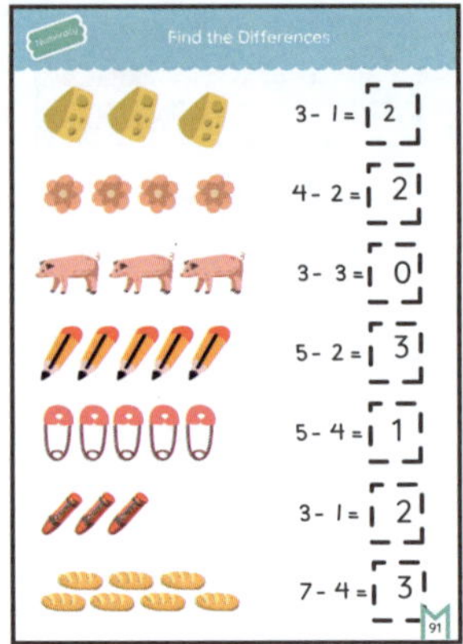

Pg no. 91

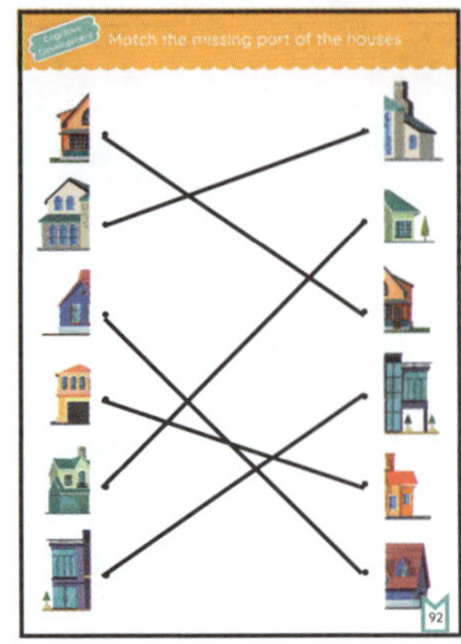

Pg no. 92

Pg no. 93

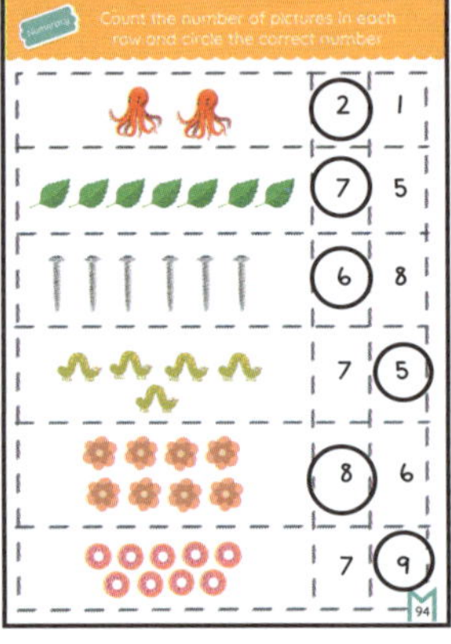

Pg no. 94

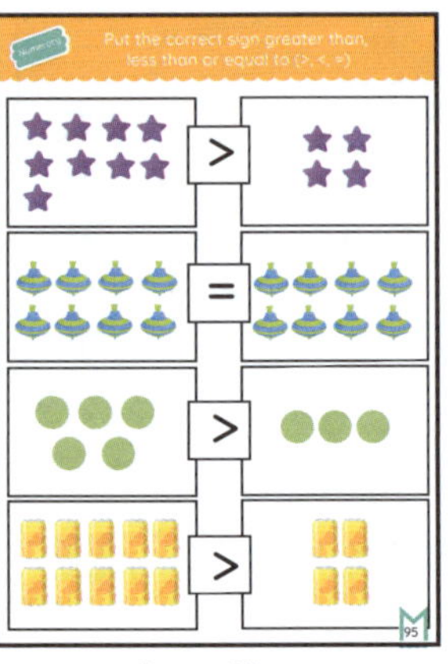

Pg no. 95

Pg no. 96

Pg no. 98

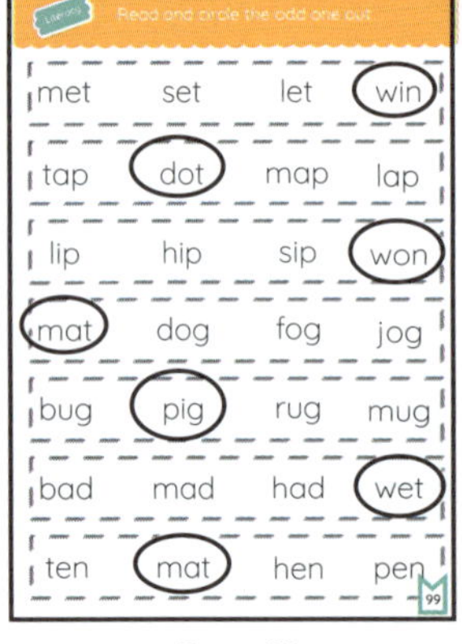

Pg no. 99

Pg no. 100

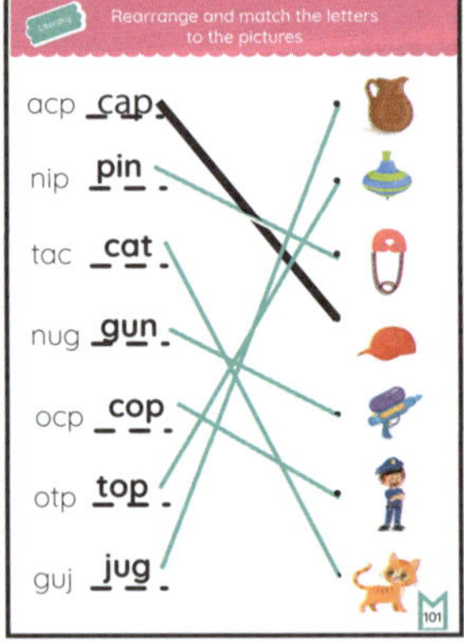

Pg no. 101

Pg no. 102

Pg no. 103

Pg no. 104

Pg no. 105

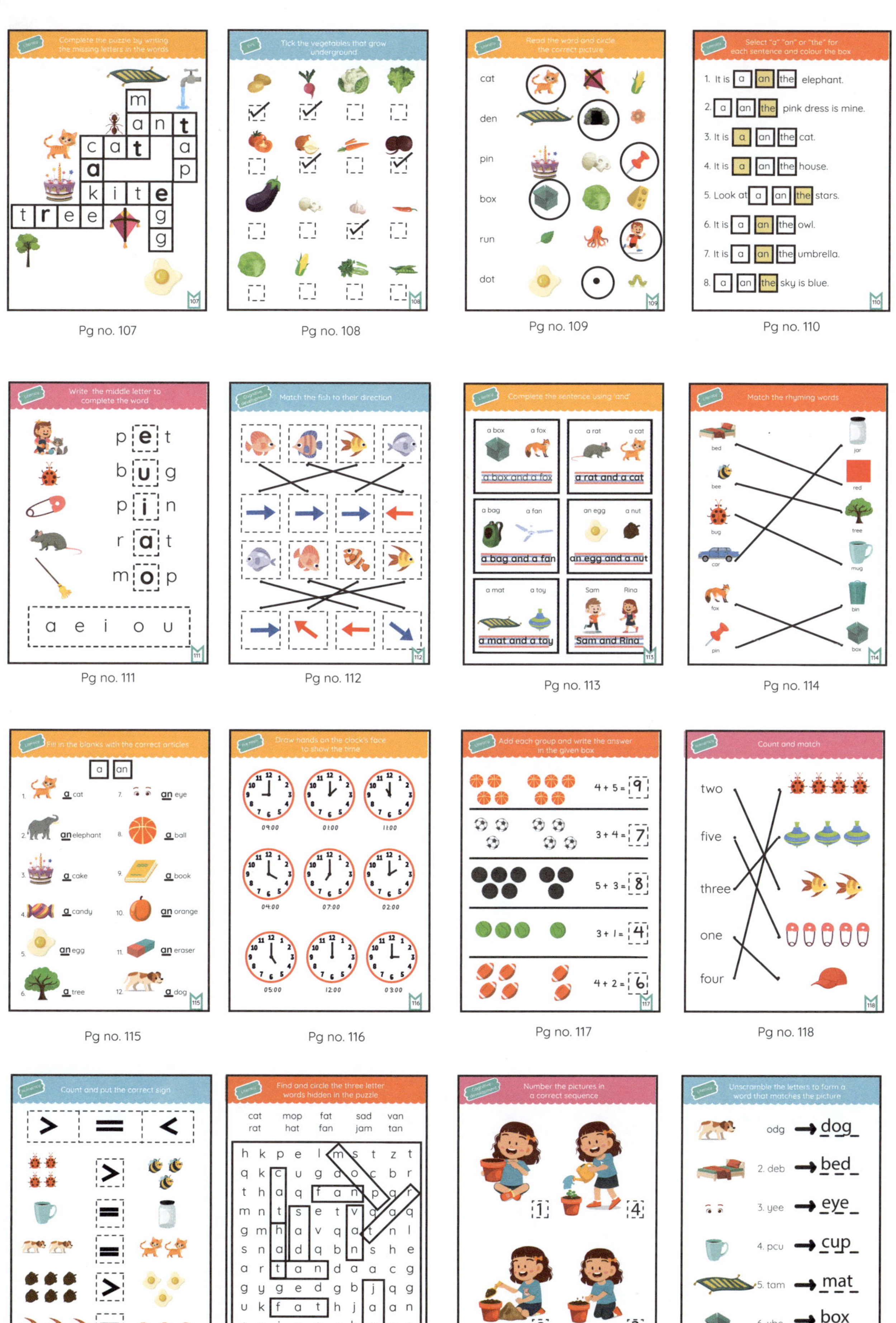
Pg no. 107

Pg no. 108

Pg no. 109

Pg no. 110

Pg no. 111

Pg no. 112

Pg no. 113

Pg no. 114

Pg no. 115

Pg no. 116

Pg no. 117

Pg no. 118

Pg no. 119

Pg no. 121

Pg no. 122

Pg no. 123

Work Space

CHAMPAK
CERTIFICATE
of Completion
THIS CERTIFICATE IS PROUDLY PRESENTED TO
for sucessful completion of K+ Activities in
little fingers Big Brains
Date
Signature